Memoirs
of the s o u l

NAN PHIFER

WALKING STICK PRESS
CINCINNATI, OHIO
www.writersdigest.com

Memoirs of the Soul: Writing Your Spiritual Autobiography. © 2002 by Nan Phifer. Manufactured in the United States of America. All rights reserved. No part of this book may be reproduced in any form or by any electronic or mechanical means including information storage and retrieval systems without permission in writing from the publisher, except by a reviewer, who may quote brief passages in a review. Published by Walking Stick Press, an imprint of F&W Publications, Inc., 1507 Dana Avenue, Cincinnati, Ohio 45207. (800) 289-0963. First edition.

Visit our Web site at www.writersdigest.com for information on more resources for writers.

To receive a free weekly e-mail newsletter delivering tips and updates about writing and about Writer's Digest products, register directly at our Web site at http:// newsletters.fwpublications.com.

06   05   04   03   02   5   4   3   2   1

Library of Congress Cataloging-in-Publication Data

Phifer, Nan
    Memoirs of the soul: writing your spiritual autobiography / by Nan Phifer.
        p.   cm.
    Includes bibliographical references and index.
    ISBN 1-58297-080-7 (alk. paper)
    1. Spiritual biography—Authorship. 2. Spiritual journals—Authorship. 3. Autobiography—Authorship. I. Title.

    BL628.5.P55   2002
    808'.066158—dc21   2001046512
                                                                      CIP

Edited by Michelle Howry and Meg Leder
Designed by Sandy Conopeotis Kent
Cover by Stephanie Strang
Cover photography by Kamil Vojnar/Photonica
Production coordinated by Kristen Heller

ACKNOWLEDGMENTS

I am indebted to the people who made the writing of this book possible:

- the people who taught me: Nat Teich, director of the Oregon Writing Project at the University of Oregon, through whom I gained expertise in methods of teaching composition; Mary K. Healy, associate director of the University of California Bay Area Writing Project (BAWP), who conveyed the theory of the writing process with unusual clarity; and Keith Caldwell, also of BAWP, who provided ingenious, infallible ideas for instruction.

- the department heads at Lane Community College who encouraged my professional growth: Dick Earl, Lance Reuther, and Pat John.

- the many workshop participants, too numerous to name, who piloted the manuscript of this book, and those who allowed me to publish excerpts from their writings.

- the writers and teachers who critiqued my manuscript and made insightful suggestions: Jane Tompkins, Anne Beaufort, Susan Mosedale, Lisa Rosen, Robbie Pinter, Lowell A. Thomas, John Creger, and Doug Finn.

- the scholars who examined this book to see if I had inadvertently been insensitive to beliefs and feelings of people whose faiths I don't know well: Tamman Adi, imam and director of an Islamic Cultural Center; Ernie Rimmerman, member of a Buddhist priory; and Shobhana Rishi, authority on Hinduism. This book was also tested by shamanic practitioner, Alida Birch, and by Sharon Franklin, a musical healer.

- the publishing experts: Elizabeth Lyon, authority in preparing book proposals; and my editors at Writer's Digest Books, Michelle Howry and Meg Leder, who gently made wise suggestions.

Most of all I am grateful for the invaluable help of my son, Matthew Rendall, and my husband, Bob Phifer, who supported my endeavor in every possible way.

ABOUT THE AUTHOR

When Nan Phifer taught at the secondary and college levels, she was awarded recognition for outstanding teaching, and she wrote the textbooks *Easing Into Essays, Writing Your Life: Developing Skills Through Life Story Writing,* and *Writing for the Workplace.* She also made presentations at many national teachers conferences.

Nan is now associate director of the Oregon Writing Project at the University of Oregon. Additionally, she founded a writing workshop for teenagers at the public library in Eugene, Oregon, and she has taught creative writing to homeless youth. Through the Older Adult Services and Information System, she guides groups of retired people who write

their memoirs. In 1998 she created a new workshop, Writing the Spiritual Memoir, which is sponsored jointly by Lane Literary Guild, the Pastoral Care Department of Peace Health Medical Group, and the Oregon Writing Project at the University of Oregon.

Nan is available to teach workshops of various lengths. Contact her by e-mail at nan phifer@mac.com, or by postal mail at 2126 Kimberly Circle, Eugene, OR 97405-5820.

Photo by Owen Carey

FOREWORD

M*emoirs of the Soul* goes beyond being a how-to book on memoir writing. It takes you on a journey into your own life that will reveal aspects of your experience you never knew existed. The author gives you all the nuts and bolts—writing prompts, warm-ups, creative exercises, doing first and second drafts, suggestions for revision, instruction on how to give and get feedback, and lots of emotional support—the practical things writers need in order to get started and make progress. But the true gift of the book is the way it introduces you to yourself.

Most people who set out to write a memoir have some kind of story to tell: memories of crucial events, interpretations of their own and other people's behavior, some scenes from childhood or adolescence, perhaps a life-changing moment of realization. But the stories about ourselves we carry around in our heads often turn out to be surface accounts, convenient shorthand versions of much deeper realities. The work of writing a memoir is really the work of learning who you are. It's archaeology: dusty and dirty and sweaty, though never tedious. Mainly what it takes is courage, courage to allow your mind to take you where it wants to go, once you've started to dig. That's where a book like this comes in. It's written by a person who has taken the journey herself and who has accompanied many other people on the way. With her, you are in good hands.

Gently and respectfully, Nan Phifer takes on the role of guide, asking you questions no one has ever put to you before, leading you to places in your own psyche you had never visited, opening landscapes of your history that you had never glimpsed, making you aware of dimensions of your being you had not realized were there. You do the work yourself but she is there to show you the way. If you follow her leads faithfully, she will take you very far. And even if you don't, you'll come away from this book with a different sense of yourself, of who you've been and who you might become.

Jane Tompkins, Ph.D.
University of Illinois in Chicago

TABLE OF CONTENTS

PART ONE

The Vision and the Plan

PART TWO

The Quest

PART ONE

The Vision and the Plan

CHAPTER ONE
Voyage of the Soul

External facts about a life can be researched generations later, but the inner life is irrevocably lost unless written during one's lifetime.

A Grand Voyage

This book will enable you to record the voyage, not of your ego, but of your soul. Public records sketch the statistics of your existence, while photographs, certificates, and documents show how you appear to others and what you accomplished. However, unless you reveal the feelings and thoughts you had when you were filled with love, grief, satisfaction, longing—the great sweep of feelings that shape your soul—few people will ever truly know you. This book will help you identify the vital elements of your inner life and write about them. Furthermore, the chapters you are about to write will not only produce a lasting, written account, but in the very process of writing, you are likely to discover previously unrecognized dimensions of spirituality in your life.

The word *spiritual* comes from the Latin word *spiritus*, meaning "breath," "breath of god," "inspiration." *Spiritual* as used in this book refers to the essential and activating principle at the center of your being, your intangible essence. It encompasses but is not limited to experiences traditionally thought of as religious. It refers to your inner life, the part of yourself at your vital core and the animating force within you.

> The further limits of our being plunge, it seems to me, into an altogether other dimension of existence from the sensible and merely "understandable" world. Name it the mystical region, or the supernatural region, whichever you choose. So far as our ideal impulses originate in this region (and most of them do originate in it, for we find them possessing us in a way for which we cannot articulately account), we belong to it in a more intimate sense than that in which we belong to the visible world,

for we belong in the most intimate sense wherever our ideals belong.

WILLIAM JAMES

AMERICAN PHILOSOPHER AND PSYCHOLOGIST

The very writing of your memoirs will stimulate personal, spiritual growth, for in articulating your ideals and your responses to the great events and formative influences in your life, you will reveal your values, motives, beliefs, and hopes. Just as you'll discover the things in your life that matter the most and the ways you've worked to advance them, you may also show the price you paid when they were ignored. Your personal traits and patterns will emerge, and you'll observe characteristics from deep within yourself. Strengths and dimensions not previously appreciated will become apparent. Later, when you compile and organize the chapters of your memoirs, you may feel that you are reintegrating elements of yourself.

You'll also gain perspective on the relationships between the events and people in your life. One of the workshop participants who followed the method presented in this book suddenly exclaimed that for the first time she understood why she had married her husband; in ways she had never consciously recognized, he was like her beloved grandfather. Someone else came to realize that for years she had carried a burden of guilt for a death that was beyond her control. Such insights are not uncommon.

Life can only be understood backwards; but it must be lived forwards.

SØREN KIERKEGAARD

DANISH PHILOSOPHER AND RELIGIOUS THINKER

First and foremost, the exploration of your spiritual life through writing will be a great adventure. Your writing will help clarify the meaning and purpose in your life, as well as reveal its underlying spiritual dimensions. If you wish, you will also produce a lasting, edited, well-written book of which you can be proud, a book that opens your life to the people who are dearest to you and makes possible communication and understanding that would otherwise never exist.

Earlier Voyagers

The first known spiritual autobiography in Western writings is *Confessions* by Saint Augustine. Subsequent writers include such people as Boethius, Jean-Jacques Rousseau, Thomas Merton, C.S. Lewis, Elie Wiesel, Harvey Cox, James Baldwin, Karen Armstrong, Alfred Kazin, and Maxine Hong Kingston. As you write your own memoirs you'll join an honorable tradition.

Memoirs are different from autobiographies. Autobiographies present broad overviews, while memoirs focus on only the hours and minutes that are keen in our lives—the times when we are most alive, when experiences penetrate to the quick. In these moments we define ourselves; the ways we respond reveal our souls. At such times—times of joy or crisis or profound contentment—our individuality emerges distinctly, and we sometimes have a sense of context beyond ourselves.

If you wish to extend your memoirs into an autobiography, you can supplement the critical core of chapters this book will guide you in writing by adding narrative data about external events. That addition will not be difficult. The memoirs you'll write at this time will give heart and soul to your autobiography and will ensure that it is engaging.

Memoirs are also different from journals. They are more selective. Memoirists focus on the most significant experiences in their lives and then organize their chapters in a sequence that tells a story; journals tend to be logs or records of daily growth, musings, and insights. Memoirs, because of their story structure, feel whole rather than fragmentary. Memoirists often want to edit and revise the first draft and have it proofread. They select photographs and other documents to insert, and they construct a book. Memoirs are usually more polished than journals and can become an art form, a type of literature. They're suitable for publication, and they make extraordinary gifts.

The Itinerary

You'll find your way to the recesses of your soul by first writing about the experiences, people, and places most important in your life. Each chapter of this guide provides a strategy to help you identify those elements and readily write about them. Writing "prompts," starters for sentences that lead into your memories, will guide you to the times when you were filled with significant emotions. After you've written rough drafts, you may choose to examine them in light of questions suggested for reflection on the topic. The reflections will help you perceive spiritual aspects such as compassion, transformation, uncanny insight, grace, and times when you were imbued with strength, were in communion with something beyond yourself, or when you sensed the divine. You may find that your writing already implicitly reveals such dimensions, or you may decide to add insights based on the reflections suggested in this book.

As you proceed through this book, you will not write chronologically. The memoirs you're about to write won't focus on where you were born, what schools you attended, or where you've lived. Other documents do that. In this book you'll write about your inner life, the heart of your being, your essence. Not until after you've collected a series of writings will you organize them—possibly chronologically, possibly some other way. The last chapter of this book suggests ways to arrange your chapters and write satisfying conclusions.

Because your approach will be to write about the critical experiences in your life rather than to render a chronological account, your writing will never plod. Because you'll not begin with "I was born . . . ," and then cite many not very interesting facts, your chapters will be compelling from the first pages. Readers will feel involved as they move from one important and dramatic aspect of your life to another. Most of us wish we could see into the hearts of those we love, and we certainly would like to look back into the souls of our ancestors. Through your writing you will share the most interesting aspects of yourself with your descendants and all other readers of your memoirs.

Travel Plans

A Glance at the Map

Many thoughtful people would like to write about their most meaningful experiences, but they don't know where to begin or how to proceed. Because the undertaking seems overwhelming, they procrastinate and write little or nothing. However, by following the steps suggested in this book, you will produce a collection of writings about your inner life.

Progression From Outer to Inner

Each chapter provides step-by-step directions to assure that inexperienced writers, as well as those with experience, can produce writing of high quality. Chapters are ordered to progress from subjects easiest to write about and share with others to subjects that might be daunting if not preceded by the earlier chapters.

The early chapters in this book begin with your outer life—the people, places, and events that shaped you. Although you'll select subjects from those accessible, factual realms, a series of questions will help you reflect on and write introspectively about the spiritual dimensions of those realms. Later chapters will enable you to write directly about your deepest emotions such as love, suffering, and ecstasy. If you've already written a reflective family history, you may prefer to skip ahead to the advanced chapters. Write in the order that best serves your purpose.

The course your voyage will follow will not be linear. Autobiographies tend to be linear, starting with birth and moving year by year to the time when the autobiography was written. Your memoirs, however, will spiral inward, moving from your outer life toward your inner life. If the word *voyage* brings images of ocean travel to your mind, you must now broaden your concept of the word, for voyages can be over land and into space as well. Visualize the map for your journey as a great labyrinth in space.

The Labyrinth Map

Labyrinths, or mazes, are ancient patterns of paths along which one progresses from an opening at the outer edge into lanes that circle, turn back, resume direction, and make unexpected twists, all the while bringing the walker from the outer entrance toward the center. One of the earliest labyrinths was constructed in Egypt for the tomb of King Perabsen, circa 3400 B.C. A well-known mythological labyrinth was in the Cretan palace where Theseus killed the Minotaur. Indoor and outdoor labyrinths have been built all over the world. The drawing shows the design of a labyrinth paved with blue and white stones in the Cathedral of Chartres, completed in the thirteenth century in France.

Medieval labyrinths were thought of as paths leading us to our own spiritual centers. In a similar way, your writing will lead you from your outer life into your spiritual center. Moreover, as walkers in a physical labyrinth can turn back to retrace their steps and linger along the way, you too may return to earlier chapters to write about more of the many topics you will have generated. Unlike the walkers of labyrinths, you'll not return the way you entered. When you've written into the heart of your memoirs, you will have arrived at your destination.

People who walk through physical labyrinths report surprise at the twists, turns, and resulting feelings of disorientation that frequently produce insights and discoveries. Upon reaching the center, many walkers experience a soothing sense of wholeness and balance. As your writing moves from your outer to your inner life, may you gain insights, make discoveries, and arrive at a sense of balance and wholeness.

An Easy Launch

Prompts will evoke your flow of words. Always feel free to rephrase the writing prompts to fit your individual life and way of speaking. When workshop participants first consider the prompts, they typically react blankly for a few minutes, then begin to write haltingly, and soon accelerate into a flow of writing. Strive to scrawl a rapid rough draft without pausing to consider what you're saying. Writing that springs uncensored from the subconscious onto the page is often revealing and insightful. One workshop participant said, "Nan, your prompts are like a can opener." Always allow the flow of your writing to take you wherever it goes; when it strays far from the prescribed subject, you may make stunning discoveries. The prompts in this book are simply catalysts. No matter what you do with them, you're "doing it right."

If you use this book in the company of other writers, you'll find their drafts to be more stimulating than any written prompt could be. Upon hearing what fellow writers have written, you'll often think, "Yes, of course!" and immediately know what in your own life must be told that would otherwise go unnoticed. To provide you with inspiration, ideas, and examples, this book contains excerpts from the drafts of many people who, like you, are composing their memoirs.

～

A writer is not so much someone who has something to say as he is someone who has found a process that will bring about new things he would not have thought of had he not started to say them.
WILLIAM STAFFORD
POET LAUREATE OF OREGON

This book provides the process.

CHAPTER TWO

Modus Operandi

We now know that to write well, we must be free to write badly. In the past, a common misconception stymied aspiring writers. They assumed that as they wrote they should choose the right words and spell and punctuate correctly. Those writers did not differentiate between a rough draft and a final draft.

Writers were liberated when it was shown that the best first drafts were filled with errors because we focused on what we were saying, not on how we were saying it. The first draft should capture ideas while they flit through our minds. We must not turn our attention from *what* we are writing to *how* we are writing because if we pause, our thoughts escape. While we puzzle over word choices and spellings, the rich feelings and ideas within us slip away. We must write quickly in order to include everything we have to tell.

The messy first draft, a rough draft, is later revised and proofread, but first the writer tries to be sure the ideas are complete and clear. The best way to do this is to hear the draft. We can read it to an attentive, nonjudgmental friend. We can ask someone to read it aloud to us, or we can read it aloud to ourselves. Any of these techniques affords perspective. Inevitably, we hear phrases that don't sound right, and we even "hear" what we inadvertently left out. Sometimes we hear that the impression made by the writing is not what we intended. Once we know what needs to be fixed, we can add to, change, rearrange, or delete what we wrote. As we do this, we're still working on content and should not be distracted by the mechanics of spelling, punctuation, and grammar. When we hear what we have written, we gain a new perspective, we see our vision from an outside angle, we reenvision it.

To write introspectively, memoirists need the freedom to make mistakes with content as well as with mechanics. After a draft is completed, it's not unusual for the writer to read it, reconsider, and conclude that the account gave the wrong impression or was somehow untrue to the experience. Memoirists, like philosophers and the other writers who discover as they compose, need freedom to err and revise as they write.

Writers who work together in critiquing groups read their first drafts to each other, hear how the drafts sound, and ask each other for suggestions. Writers working alone benefit from reading their rough drafts aloud to themselves or to the cat, or by taping them and listening to the tape. Any oral reading and listening is helpful.

After you have revised the content of your rough draft, then you're ready to proofread it. If you're using a computer, use its spell-checker. If you're uncertain about your choice of words, punctuation, or paragraphing, you can ask someone to proofread for you. However, unless you plan to publish your memoirs, don't let concerns about mechanics be overriding and certainly don't let them stop you from your undertaking. Your close friends and family will be glad to have your memoirs, whether or not they contain mechanical errors.

The following steps of the writing process will be helpful as you write each chapter. Mark this page with a bookmark so you can readily refer to it.

Starting with chapter four, each chapter will begin with a preliminary warm-up writing, followed by a second writing. The warm-up writings will limber up your mind and stimulate your fluency, they'll serve to propel your writing, and usually they'll initiate subjects you'll want to develop into chapters. If you are writing independently on your own schedule, you'll probably want to revise, proofread, and write the final version of your warm-up writing before going on to the second writing. However, if you are working alongside other writers, you'll want to set the first rough draft aside for later completion and proceed as a group to the second writing. The first steps of the writing process—gathering ideas, listening, and responding to rough drafts—are interactive. People writing in groups will want to do those steps while they are together, but you can complete the last steps—revising, proofreading, and writing an improved final draft—apart from your group.

Some topics presented in this book develop better for certain individuals than for others. Writers are often surprised to find a prompt that didn't at first appear promising, leading into a full, rich chapter, while

THE STEPS OF THE WRITING PROCESS

This book uses the following approach, which usually facilitates good writing. If it does not help you, feel free to alter it. It is meant as a general, flexible guide, not a constraining formula.

1. Gather ideas. Each chapter will help you use memory aids: photographs, documents, souvenirs, maps, lists, graphs. You'll find that your life abounds with subjects. The idea-gathering strategies in this book will generate many more seeds for stories than you can use the first time you go through a chapter. You'll store lists of ideas for future chapters in a "greenhouse" file.

2. Tell a friend or writing partner the story you are considering writing. By narrating orally before you write, you'll organize your ideas and find the words you want.

3. Scrawl a quick rough draft, skipping lines so you'll have room to revise. Putting fluency first, ignore spelling and punctuation; you'll proofread for mechanics later. Number pages. Dare to ramble. Pursue your thoughts without concern for mechanical correctness.

4. Listen to the rough draft. Read it aloud to yourself, to a dear friend, or to a response group. Any listening is helpful. You'll find out if you expressed what you intended to convey.

5. Revise the rough draft if you wish. You may want to clarify, restate, or add information. Your revision may or may not be influenced by listeners' responses.

6. If you're concerned about punctuation, grammar, or spelling, consider asking someone to proofread for you. If you write your final drafts on a word processor, take advantage of the spell-checker.

7. Handwrite, type, or keyboard a final draft.

another rough draft may remain meager. Because this book approaches each chapter subject in two different ways, at least one of your drafts will thrive and flourish, and usually both will. The second writing is designed to develop more fully than the first, but the warm-up writing sometimes supersedes it.

Your Greenhouse File

Keep a manila folder or a section of notebook as a "greenhouse" file. This "holding bed" is a place to store ideas for later chapters and a place to "plant" drafts you don't like, stunted beginnings, and even unexpected inspirations. Sometimes an idea forms when we don't have time to put it in writing. Store the idea, the seed, in your greenhouse file along with the various beginnings that need germination time. Later you can take out whatever looks promising and give it a new opportunity to flourish in whatever form it takes.

The Rough Draft

A successful technique for writing rough drafts is to skip lines so you'll have space to rewrite sentences and insert new ones. Packages of ordinary, lined notebook paper are ideal, but some writers prefer cheap spiral notebooks or legal pads. Choose any sort of paper on which you can skip lines, make insertions, and write error-strewn, impulsive drafts. Before beginning to write, make an *X* in the left margin of every other line as a reminder to write on alternating lines. You'll feel that you're using lots of paper, but you'll need room to write in changes and additions.

Write on only one side of the paper so you can later cut pages apart to insert and rearrange paragraphs. You cannot "cut and paste" if you write on the back.

Number pages and even identify them with a chapter number or subject word so you can reassemble them more easily if they become shuffled. Of course, if you are using a computer many of these arrangements will automatically be taken care of for you.

We all have our individual habits and quirks and may not feel fluent unless we approach our writing in a familiar way. Thus, consider the advice in this book and then do what will work best for you.

The Final Draft: A Lasting Book

Not every voyager cares about creating a book. The expedition, the discoveries that come from the writing itself, is the great adventure.

You are no less a traveler if you do not produce a book for others to read; however, many voyagers do find satisfaction in polishing their first drafts and leaving a lasting account.

Just as you would value a book written by one of your ancestors centuries ago, the memoir you are writing now may someday be of keen interest to your great-great-great-grandchild. You may even decide to publish copies for a broader community.

Ordinary paper becomes brittle and crumbly after about thirty years, but acid-free paper will last for three hundred years. You can buy it at stationery or art supply stores. The store where you buy paper may sell several qualities that range in price, but the least expensive will serve well. The important thing is that the paper be labeled "acid-free."

Handwrite, type, or keyboard your final version onto acid-free paper. When you make copies of your memoirs, you may need to bring your own acid-free paper to the copy shop.

Leave space to insert photographs, clippings, and documents that you want to include. Those pictures and other items will be preserved when copied onto the acid-free paper. If you like to sketch, consider embellishing your book with drawings and ornamentation.

Office supply stores carry a variety of binders, some inexpensive and some costly. Choose according to your preference and means, and consider making copies of your memoirs for the people to whom you feel close. It is the most personal gift you can give and will be increasingly treasured by the people who come to know you through your book, perhaps long after your lifetime.

Obstacles You May Encounter

Procrastination

"Tomorrow. Tomorrow I'll really sit down and write. Next week. Next year. After I do the dishes, mow the lawn, fix the faucet, watch a TV show."

To be able to write your spiritual memoirs, you must first be convinced of the worth of your undertaking. If you feel dubious about it, then you'll give priority to routine chores and passive pleasures. Sitting down to write won't just happen; you have to resolve to make it happen.

Many writers benefit from keeping a schedule. They reserve certain hours of every day or every week for writing. To succeed with a schedule, to be able to decline tempting invitations and distractions without hesitation, you must first believe in the merits of your project. Then earnestly ask your family and friends not to interrupt you during your time for writing.

Another way many writers conquer procrastination is by scheduling regular meetings with a small group of other writers. At these meetings everyone reads from works in progress. Knowing that fellow members expect everyone to bring a draft to read provides strong incentive to produce writing. For suggestions about how to write with companions or colleagues, see chapter twenty-seven.

A rigid writing schedule and regular meetings are arbitrary structures, but they do help many successful writers accomplish their goals. If we wait for the muse to whisper in our ears, we may never do more than intend to get around to writing tomorrow or next week or next year.

Honor the grand voyage of writing your spiritual memoirs. Most people have never considered doing what you are about to do. It isn't frivolous or easy or trivial. Close the door to the room in which you write, unplug the telephone, breathe deeply and slowly, and in a prayerful manner approach each day's writing. Award-winning science fiction writer Bruce Holland Roger has attached a motto to his computer that says, "I am an angel in disguise writing a holy text." He chuckles as he tells this, yet he believes in the significance of his work. You are undertaking the writing of your spiritual memoirs, a profoundly meaningful project, so find symbols for your work space, create rituals for yourself, respect your writing schedule, and your success will not be waylaid by procrastination.

Negative Criticism

Criticism from contemporaries is of greater concern to memoirists and autobiographers than to most other writers. We worry about what our families will think and about how listeners and readers will evaluate not only the writing but the lives we've lived and ourselves as individuals. These worries can become debilitating. If we dwell on them our writing will be stunted.

For memoirs to be genuine and deep, your writing must be as candid as possible. Write your first draft for yourself alone. Write honestly. If your writing is intended only for yourself and, perhaps, a few selected friends, then you are free of concern. However, if you are writing for members of your family, for your community, or for broad publication, at a later time, before you write your final draft, you can decide whether to edit out parts that might cause harm or distress.

Frequently, the information we feel guilty about revealing actually has the effect of eliciting sympathy from readers. For the first time, readers may understand our intentions, our problems, and our regrets. They usually respond with compassion.

At all stages of your writing you'll have the option of sharing or not sharing your chapters with friends and fellow writers. If you are writing with a partner or workshop participants, you may always say, "This time I'll pass" when it is your turn to read.

Step four of the writing process suggests that you read your rough draft to listeners. So that your listeners know how to respond constructively, give them the listeners' guidelines.

If you are writing independently, respond in the recommended way to your own drafts. Acknowledge their strengths and then stop to won-

---

GUIDELINES FOR LISTENERS

- Listen with a nonjudgmental, open mind.
- Listen to learn.
- Remain totally, unfailingly confidential about what you will hear.

To respond constructively to the draft you hear:
1. Tell what you like about the writing. Point out a strength in either the content or manner of writing.
2. Ask a question about something the writer did not tell.

Now you, the listener, have said enough. Unless the writer asks your opinion about something else, say no more.

der what questions a listener who doesn't know you might have. We often inadvertently omit essential information.

Groups of writers who carefully follow the guidelines for listeners ensure that the response group is safe, supportive, and constructive for all writers. This procedure has been repeatedly tested and found reliable. If the ideas of a fellow writer grieve or offend you, then do not respond at all. Simply remain silent.

Bad feelings have occasionally festered in groups that have not followed these guidelines. You'll use them throughout this book, so please mark the guidelines for easy reference or make copies of them.

Concern About Mechanical Correctness

Writers should never hesitate to write their memoirs because they cannot spell or do not understand grammar and punctuation. Poignant, priceless memoirs have been written by unschooled writers. The thoughts and feelings of the writer are what matter most. The people who love you will overlook or will notice your mechanical errors; either way, they will be grateful to you for proceeding to write your memoirs.

Look at the proofreading tips in chapter thirty for ways to proofread your rough drafts before writing your final versions.

Questions About Regionalisms

Memoirists sometimes wonder if they should drop their regionalisms. The answer is no! The locale where you grew up has flavored who you are. If, when you talk, you "reckon" or "hanker," and you call the frying pan a "spider" or use "gum bands" instead of rubber bands, use these words. To whitewash them out of your memoirs would be to erase a part of yourself. If you were writing a technical report or an academic essay, then you would replace your regionalisms, but if you were doing that kind of writing you wouldn't be writing about yourself.

The daughter of one writer said she intended to read only the first chapter of her father's memoirs before she went to bed. However, when she began reading she "could just hear Dad talking," and she was unable put his book down until she had read all of it.

Final Preparations

Notice the suggested readings in chapter twenty-eight. This list is a resource for people who write alone or with informal groups, as well as for people who teach or enroll in memoir-writing classes. As you scan the authors' names, be aware that by writing your spiritual memoirs, you are joining an esteemed company.

Memoirs of the Soul is a manual, a travelers' guide to follow step-by-step to the center of your spiritual labyrinth. Along the way you'll find two kinds of guideposts. One series simply identifies where you are along the steps of the writing process. The indicators telling what to do next function as "You Are Here" signs. The other set of directions will lead you through the labyrinth. If you sometimes feel jerked about, have faith that the twists and turns you'll follow will eventually bring you to a place you could not have reached by a direct path; each lane you explore will prepare you for the next.

Ready to Embark

You are about to launch forth on a grand adventure, a voyage of discovery through writing. As you reflect on the most important dimensions of your life, you'll gain new perspectives and insights. Moreover, because questing writers don't know exactly what they'll find until they write, you're likely to surprise yourself. You'll write both to discover and to record your very essence, your soul.

Whether you write independently, with a partner, or as part of a writing group depends on your own preference and circumstances. Some people prefer the privacy and quietness of writing individually, while other people find interaction with fellow writers to be stimulating and helpful. If you will write with colleagues or a friend, please see chapter twenty-seven at this time. Used by yourself or in collaboration with fellow writers, this guide will enable you to write profound and powerful spiritual memoirs.

You're ready to make a spiritual voyage, and if you wish, to produce memoirs that will enable the people you love to see into your heart and mind. Please step aboard.

PART TWO

The Quest

CHAPTER THREE

Subjects for Your Memoirs

The heart has its reasons, which reason does not know.

BLAISE PASCAL

FRENCH RELIGIOUS THINKER, MATHEMATICIAN, PHYSICIST

May I use the pronoun *I*?
Am I important enough to write about my own life?
Do I have enough to say?
Yes to all these questions.

One of the first questions some beginning memoirists ask is "May I use the pronoun *I*?" People who ask this question probably were instructed by their teachers to avoid using the first person, but the kinds of assignments being taught to them were probably reports and impersonal essays. Memoirs are a different genre. The pronoun *I* is correct for all personal writing.

Deeply moving, meaningful memoirs have been written by people who are not famous or important in a public way. The writing of spiritual memoirs has nothing to do with celebrity status or worldly achievements. Memoirs are about our ideals and intentions, the longings and laughter that have filled our hearts, the love we have felt, the compassion we have received and given, and the moments when we have been graced, and when we have transcended ourselves. These experiences have little or nothing to do with status. As you write reflectively on your inner life, you will discover your spiritual importance.

You have much to say. An idea-gathering exercise in each chapter of this book will bring forth such an array of significant personal subjects that you'll be surprised at how many important memories you have to write about. Each topic could develop into a chapter or a section of a chapter. This chapter will prove to you that your life is so filled with subjects, you'll have to be selective.

The first step of the writing process is to capture ideas. Idea-gathering strategies in each chapter of this book will draw key words from your life, words that identify the text of your life.

One way to discover subjects for your memoir is to name the people, places, activities, things and experiences you "hold in your heart."

On a sheet of 8½" × 11" (22 cm × 28 cm) notebook paper, draw a valentine-shaped heart large enough to fill the page. Don't be concerned

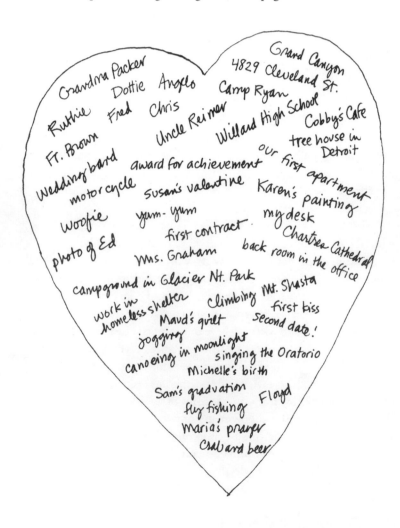

if it's lopsided or askew; real hearts aren't valentine shaped anyway. If you are anatomically minded, then draw your heart more egg shaped, the shape of a real human heart.

If your heart starts to overflow as you fill it with words, write on the back of your page or draw a second heart on another page.

Inside the heart, list or name at random the following:

People who have been important to you

- They may be alive or dead, young or old.
- Their impact on you may have been good or bad.
- You may have been any age when they were important.
- Remember parents, friends, lovers, enemies, colleagues, employers, children, and other people about whom you've felt emotion.

The idea-gathering strategies throughout this book are only that, strategies. If they prompt thoughts that go beyond suggestions in this book, they are working well. The strategies are like flint whose purpose is to ignite your own memory and thought. Freely change or deviate from any suggestion in this book at any time.

When Geri Meyers filled in her heart during a workshop, she asked if a dog could be entered under "people." The answer is yes! Every idea for writing that arises from your life can be included. Later in this chapter you'll read what Geri wrote.

Places where significant events in your life occurred

- Geographic locations
    homes
    parks
    sanctuaries
    your personal retreat
    a meeting place
    a place where a dramatic event occurred
    a place where you were very happy or miserable
    If you think of big formations like cities and mountain ranges
        and seashores, name the particular spot in their midst where
        you were.
- Institutions
    schools

      camps

      places of worship

      work sites

      hospitals

- Interior spaces

      a bedroom

      a certain kitchen

      a childhood place where you played or hid

      a place like the backseat of the old Ford

Things you have valued or would be sorry to lose

- Belongings that have sentimental value

      gifts

      something made by hand

      an item associated with an important occasion

      letters

      a trinket that reminds you of a good time

- Possessions that represent achievements

      awards and trophies

      things you worked for and saved your money to buy

- Items that provide pleasure

      musical instruments

      sports equipment

      particular books

      shop or gardening tools, even a birdhouse

Activities or experiences important to you

- Physical

      hiking

      camping

      running

      walking the dog

      stacking wood

      playing ball games

      cycling

      swimming

      exercising

- Intellectual

      reading
      conversing
      writing
      taking classes
      teaching
      studying
      thinking
      discovering

- Emotional times
  - bliss or wretchedness
  - consuming fear or dread or anxiety
  - tender love, peace, compassion, hope, longing
- Religious feelings
  - rituals you observe
  - meditation and personal prayers
  - experiences associated with beliefs and doubts
  - times of compassion and of grace
  - moments of transcendence

After you've filled in your heart choose subjects for your memoirs. Looking at the words you've written inside the heart, circle those that could be topics for chapters or parts of chapters. In choosing subjects, trust your intuition. Some subjects pulse with more importance than others. A topic your family or acquaintances might consider important may not be as meaningful to you as other subjects. Be guided by your feelings.

From the subjects you circled, choose the one you feel most inclined to write about today. It doesn't need to be the most significant subject or the most spiritual. In the following weeks and months you'll have time to write about as many of these subjects as you wish. The best way to select the one to write about at this moment is to follow your enthusiasm; that's where your energy hovers.

~

John Pierce remembered a particular blind date as an emotional and important event. He married Lura four years after meeting her, and they are still lovingly married. Here is an excerpt from John's memoirs.

I first met her on a blind date. I had many blind dates. They were my norm. I joined a fraternity my freshman year in college, and all pledges were required to have at least two dates per week. Where I went to school I knew no one, for I had moved to Oklahoma the day following my graduation from high school. Being rather shy in the boy-meets-girl category, blind dates became my only alternative.

I breathed a sigh of relief when Christmas break came. It meant a two-week reprieve from that terrible awkwardness. However, one of my fraternity brothers came home with me to Bartlesville. The girl he was dating lived there, and my house was a convenient stopover for his romance.

Gene felt sorry for me. So did the young woman he was dating, and she had a friend. "You'll like her, she has a great personality," Tolly said. (I'd been through this before.) "There is a Christmas dance, and we can arrange a date for you. Besides, Lura needs a date, too."

"What's her name?"

"Lura."

"You mean Lora? . . . Laura?"

"No, Lura. It's a family name I think."

"How tall is she?"

"Five nine."

"Too tall!"

"Come on, John. You'll like her. She's really funny."

I sighed. "Oh, well, I guess it's something to do." Hanging up, I mumbled to myself, "I really don't want to do this again."

On that fateful night, Gene picked up Tolly first, and the three of us drove to Keeler Street to pick up my tall blind date with the different name. The driveway at 1940 Keeler led to a big, white, two-story house on a corner lot. On the left of the drive stood a glass greenhouse filled with all kinds of flowering plants that her mother and father grew as a hobby, and to make it a paying proposition, some were sold to the community. The walkway from the drive led to the back door over which a porch light brightly burned. I felt apprehensive coming to the back door to ring the bell.

With fear and trembling I approached, and as I reached out to push the button for the bell I thought, "Why am I doing this? Life doesn't have to be this hard." I rang it anyway and waited what seemed like the longest and also the shortest wait of my life.

There she was, all five feet nine inches of her. Beautiful! ("Why does she need a blind date?") Large brown eyes; red, full lips; and a most marvelous smile!

"Yes," I thought. "Yes, indeed."

Velma Tweedie also met her spouse, Bill, on a blind date that she set up for a friend, but Velma and Bill were "taken with each other." They whispered throughout a movie the two couples had gone to see. After a year of courtship, Velma quit her job in a doctor's office to marry Bill. This is her recollection of their wedding day.

When the strains of "At Dawning" began, I emerged from the kitchen—my beautiful bride's bouquet of pink roses and stephanotis (made by my mother) was shaking. My knees were, too.

The ceremony began. The minister's voice was booming, and I tried to concentrate on what he was saying. All was quiet until my small stepsister Bonnie wailed, "I don't want Velma to leave." Then I started to cry—and, one by one—all the guests began to weep, even my former boss, our reserved and contained family doctor. All were weeping—that is, except the groom—who patiently waited for the tears to subside.

Our vows were finally sealed with the usual but damp kiss. The minister said it was the wettest wedding he'd ever witnessed.

After a beautifully planned and prepared luncheon given us by family and friends, we set off in our blue Chevrolet, with a rumble seat. We climbed the hill to the top of the picturesque rim rocks— the sun was shining, the snow was melting—and we headed for southern California on our honeymoon.

Suddenly the engine began to make queer, explosive noises and smoke poured forth. On examination we found quantities of rice on the engine. Bill swept it out, and we were on our way. . . .

～

Like Velma and John, you'll write about a vivid memory, though your story, whatever it is, will be different from theirs. You may write about a place you remember well, a person who made a difference in your life, or an experience you'll never forget. Your subject may be pleasant to remember or it could bring tears to your eyes. Choose from among the many subjects you named in your heart.

The most natural way to begin the flow of words is by telling your story before writing it. Speaking is more spontaneous than writing, so if you tell even briefly what you plan to write, you'll write with ease. If a suitable listener isn't present, imagine telling your story to someone you love or to an interested, understanding individual.

For the moment, lay your pen aside. Visualize your friend, waiting, listening, ready to hear what you will say. Notice how you would begin your story, what words you would use. Now pick up your pen and write those opening sentences on paper, knowing you can change them later. Sometimes, even sentences that aren't very good do the job well because they get you started.

Telling your story to a listener before beginning to write, or even imagining that you are telling it to a friend, will give a sincere, personal tone to your writing. It will be more appealing and readable than if you did not have a particular listener in mind, and you will make a natural transition from speaking to writing.

～

If you're writing independently, skip the boxed directions. From here on, instructions for people writing together are in boxes. (For more instruction, see chapter twenty-seven.)

If you're writing with a partner or group of writers:
- Tell either your partner or another individual in the group the story you plan to write.
- Listen while your partner tells you the story she or he plans to write.

Keep in mind the previous chapter's suggestions for writing successful first drafts. Only by writing several rough drafts on different subjects
will you acquire the habit of skipping lines and using only one side of
the paper.

Your first draft will flow more freely if you focus on content and
ignore mechanics such as spelling, punctuation, grammar, and word
choice. If you stop to wonder about those things as you are composing
your ideas, your thoughts will be interrupted. Later when you proofread
you'll attend to the mechanics of writing. Right now it's all right to
have a draft filled with mechanical errors.

One good way to begin is with the words "When I was. . . ." Let
your readers know about how old you were and something about your
circumstances. Orient them so they'll know how and where to visualize
you, and then tell the story. Quickly write whatever comes to mind. Later
you can insert additional information and make changes and corrections.

The length of each piece is determined by how much you have to tell.
You might produce an entire chapter, or you might create a series of short
sections on different topics. If you're writing alongside fellow writers, plan
to write for twenty to thirty minutes or until most people have paused.

Look back at what you've written, particularly to see if you told
about your feelings. Sometimes writers describe what happened but
forget to tell how they were affected. Revise your rough draft by insert-
ing information about your feelings.

⌐

Geri Meyers did tell how she felt when she was eight years old. She
escaped a heavy atmosphere at home by riding her emerald green bicycle
and taking her little dog, Moe, as a passenger in the wire handlebar
basket.

Geri is currently researching her family's genealogy and writing her
memoirs for her grandchildren.

*I mounted my emerald charger, a means that carried my friend
and me on an emotional cleansing. The wind washed us with an
independence and carefree spirit my parents had long forgotten. I*

searched for the freedom to experience happiness free from my parents'
anger, arguing, mistrust, and bitterness. I didn't know why they were
that way. It was all I ever knew, but I yearned to be surrounded by
joy, not heaviness. I remember at eight years old modestly expressing
my one wish to my mother . . . "I wish I could be happy for one
whole day." My parents' distance from each other permeated our
home. But on my bike I was in control of its movement and my
direction. It was different . . . it was always joyful and lightened my
burdens.

Moe was a fifteen-pound toy terrier/Pomeranian mix. His short
hair was fawn-colored with a white patch shaped like a diamond
that marked his chest, and his naturally coiled tail was tipped with
white as if dipped in paint. He looked like a soldier at attention. He
was sitting with his chest bowed out, his head erect, and his ears
straight up with attentiveness to my every word and so willing to
please me. When I spoke, I had his undivided attention, and it gave
me such a feeling of worth.

I asked him, "Would you like to take a ride?" As he stood on all
fours, his tail started to wag with an upbeat tempo, and his tongue
popped out of his mouth as he panted with anticipation of the prom-
ised outing. He lifted his feet with excitement as though the cool grass
were a bed of hot coals. It was a grand response of splendor when
others I loved didn't have time for me. My handlebars supported a
large woven wire basket. Moe was able to balance his small feet on
the wires, but I learned to make the ride more comfortable for him
by nesting the basket with my doll's blanket.

As we rode down the street with the breeze flowing over us, I had
my head tilted back, my chin pointing out, while my nostrils enjoyed
the freshness of a new day. I laughed because Moe had his head back,
eyes shut, and his ears were flapping in the wind. We both thrived
on those freeing moments and bonded with each venture.

～

After you've composed your rough draft, the next step is to listen to
it. When you hear your rough draft, you'll gain a sense of how it affects

others, whether it comes across the way you intended, and whether it's clear and complete. Professional writers usually work in critiquing groups, groups of writers who listen to each other's rough drafts and respond with their reactions and suggestions. Often they take turns meeting in their homes where they gather around the dining table or group themselves in the living room to hear and discuss their drafts. Compatible, constructive groups continue to work together for years.

If when you read your draft your listeners become confused or have questions, you'll realize what you need to do to make your story clear. If they don't share the emotion you meant to convey, you can determine where additional information is needed.

If you're writing independently, find a quiet, peaceful place where you can read aloud to yourself, undisturbed, or you might find a dear friend who's willing to listen while you read your rough draft. Some writers even tape-record their drafts so they can hear them. Reading your draft aloud, even without the benefit of listeners who respond, reveals ways you can improve it. You'll "hear" ways you can make it better.

When you read your rough draft aloud to yourself, and especially if you read it to someone else, you "viewed" it from another perspective. You reenvisioned it. The aural experience gives you insight into how to revise it. Think of the experience in your life, the actual experience you lived, as the first experience. The experience you imagined when you heard your written description is the second, and somewhat different, experience. When we hear and imagine what we wrote, we perceive discrepancies between the two experiences and "see" what we need to do to mesh them, to bring them into alignment, to make the second experience true to the first. You may wish to add information, take something out, change words or phrases, or reorganize the sequence of your telling. Make any changes that will result in your story being more understandable and accurate. Revise it.

Memoir writers often wonder if they may tell all they really experienced, thought, and felt, or if they should censor themselves. If you want to learn all you can about yourself, to really explore the depth of your soul, then write candidly and honestly. But if you are concerned about condemnation by readers or fear that what you say could harm

If you're writing with a large group, divide into subgroups of three or four and read to each other.

Most of us feel uneasy about reading aloud our writing. We feel vulnerable, knowing we could be criticized. When we made oral reports in school, our hearts probably banged and our stomachs cramped, even though those reports were about impersonal, factual information. Now you find this book recommending that you reveal personal information about significant events in your life to people you might not know well. So that your listeners understand the spirit in which they are to listen, tell them about the guidelines for listeners on page 15.

Your listeners must agree to be nonjudgmental and supportive, to listen, to learn, and to guard the confidentiality of each writer.

Respond to each rough draft you hear by:

- First, telling what you like about it. What are its strengths? What did you admire?

- Then, asking for further information. Writers often assume they've explained things they have left out. Your questions will help the writer know how to reinforce the draft.

Unless the writer asks for more suggestions, you've said enough. If the writer does ask a specific question, then try to answer it.

Your role is *not* to evaluate the actions or feelings of the writer.

someone else, then you must determine what to omit or, perhaps, alter.

One practical approach is to write the rough draft as candidly as possible, let some time pass, and later decide whether to edit any parts that concern you.

When you are satisfied that your rough draft does create the story you want to tell in the minds of listeners or readers, then you're ready to have it proofread. Our friends and families usually prefer that we write the way we speak, so concern about grammar may not be necessary.

However, if you would like help with the mechanics of standard English, ask a friend to check your:

- paragraphing
- punctuation
- selection of words
- capitalization
- spelling

If you use a computer to word process your final draft, its software probably includes a spell-checker. Take advantage of it. If you feel uneasy about your basic, overall proofreading skills, refer to the proof-reading tips in chapter thirty. The expectations of your anticipated reading audience can determine the amount of attention that you give to proofreading.

Now is the time to think of a title for your chapter. It can be as simple and straightforward as one word, or it can be fanciful. Think of Eudora Welty's title "Why I Live at the P.O.," Honoré de Balzac's "A Passion in the Desert," Dorothy Parker's "Big Blonde," and Seymour Freedgood's "Grandma and the Hindu Monk." Other intriguing titles imply answers: "The Reason I'm a Vegetarian," "Because My Watch Had Stopped," "Why I Dropped Out of High School." Ask the people who listened to your rough draft to suggest titles. Listeners are likely to name what they perceived as the theme of your chapter, suggestions that frequently provide surprising insights for the writer.

At this time you're ready to write your final draft. Remember to use acid-free paper, and if you're writing by hand, you no longer need to skip lines.

Collect final drafts of all your chapters in a box or notebook where they'll be safe. Eventually you'll organize them, make a title page, write a conclusion, and bind your pages. Chapter twenty-six explains how to assemble your own book.

The heart you filled with names of people, places, events, and impor-tant things can serve as your book's table of contents. Save it. Keep it in a loose-leaf notebook or a manila folder you think of as your green-house file. In addition to storing ideas for further chapters, this file will also be a good place to "plant" unfinished rough drafts.

You've accomplished the hardest part—getting started—which is a barrier for many people. You've made the breakthrough! You found that you have numerous possible topics, and you've gone through the process of drafting, revising, and writing a final version. If you want to write about more of the subjects you circled in your heart, do so now, following the same process.

CHAPTER FOUR

Breathing Life Into Your Writing

A writer's problem does not change. He himself changes and the world he lives in changes but his problem remains the same. It is always how to write truly and having found what is true, to project it in such a way that it becomes a part of the experience of the person who reads it.

ERNEST HEMINGWAY

AMERICAN NOVELIST AND SHORT-STORY WRITER

Certain experiences remain within us from the day when they occurred throughout the rest of our lives. They formed us. They might be as small as the overhearing of a whispered sentence, but we recorded them in our memories, and they became part of who we are. By writing about these experiences, we understand them from a new perspective and may gain insights. By sharing the aspects of our inner lives with trusted friends, we allow these people to truly know us.

This chapter demonstrates a technique for describing incidents so vividly that your readers will feel what you felt. You will write about a memorable experience in a way that will engage your readers. The next chapter will guide you through another application of the same technique. After that, you can employ it whenever you wish as you write the remaining chapters.

～

Begin with a writing warm-up. As you write this rough draft, tell whatever comes to mind and write without concern for correctness. Write for about twenty minutes, using one of the following prompts:

- A day I'll never forget . . .
- An experience that made a great impact on me was . . .
- My pulse quickened when . . .

Read aloud this rough draft. The account you've just written may be one you'll enjoy sharing with a companion; if it is not, read it aloud to yourself in a quiet, private place.

If you are writing with fellow writers, form small groups and listen to each other's drafts. Remember to listen respectfully, learn all you can, and never repeat what you will hear.

 Notice the following new response suggestion:
* **Point out a word, phrase, or sentence that remains most vivid in your mind.**
* **Then ask a question.**

Wes Flinn gathered ideas for this description of a bagpiper by first systematically analyzing his sensory memories. Wes is a writer and teacher in Eugene, Oregon, where he lives with his beautiful wife and puppy. He enjoys catching images with a camera, as well as with his pen.

> *My bride was walking toward me. I was unsure and shaky; thankfully, the bagpipes tethered me to the ground with tones of celebration. I was drawn back to the day we chose our piper.*
>
> *We found him at the end of a maze of rural Massachusetts roads: a staunch conservative with a raggedy, unruly beard and bits of lunch still clinging to the crevices between his teeth. He was a man fighting passionately for gun rights and freedom to do what the hell he likes at home. A self-proclaimed Rush Limbaugh listener and grower of his own food and hops for brewing, he also created his own kilts and piping garb. He walked around his yard, pipes blaring, letting their sounds of marching and the history of battlegrounds fill us with excitement and anticipation. Amy looked down and plucked a four-leaf clover from the overgrown grass by the woodpile. How can you turn your nose at such a clear sign? We hired John on the spot and were never sorry.*

Notice how effectively Wes included small details—the bits of food between the piper's teeth and the four-leaf clover underfoot.

To prepare for your second rough draft, think of an experience you would like to relive, or one you wish had not happened, or one that made a difference in the way you think or feel about yourself. The subject you choose can be either positive or negative. The episode may have been traumatic or exhilarating, or it could be memorable for quiet, personal reasons. Any experience you've replayed in your mind is one that has become part of you and one that can be an excellent subject choice.

A way to identify significant experiences is to list:

Times when
- your heart pounded
- your stomach tightened
- your skin tingled
- you held your breath
- you wept with joy, relief, grief, or sympathy

Experiences you would like
- to relive
- to erase

The best time for planning a book is while you're doing the dishes.
AGATHA CHRISTIE
ENGLISH WRITER OF DETECTIVE FICTION

~

Select one intense experience from your list to write about today, and then place this list of subjects in your greenhouse folder.

You can use the technique you are about to follow anytime you want to convey an experience to readers so they will live it with you.

Write your first name in the middle of a sheet of paper 8½″ × 11″ (22 cm × 28 cm) or larger.

Think of a particular moment in the experience you're about to describe. Then, in your mind, locate yourself in the precise spot where you were. With pen over your page, imagine that your page is an overview of the setting, with yourself in the middle where your name is written.

First use your sense of vision. Write the names of things you see from your location. Place the names of the things you can touch close to your name in the middle. Place the distant things out near the edges of the paper. Name everything you remember seeing. (See the next page for an example.)

When you have finished naming everything you saw, then name the sounds you heard. Write names of distant, background sounds near the edges of the paper and the names of nearby sounds close to your name. You could write in larger letters any predominant sounds or sounds that startled you. If someone said something, write the spoken words with quotation marks around them. If you said something, quote yourself.

Your paper is now becoming spattered with words. The more crowded it becomes, the more material you'll have at your disposal. So far you've analyzed only two senses, sight and hearing; as you continue, your page is going to become crammed with words. Not all of the following suggestions will apply to your experience, so just pass over those that don't work. Suggestions that don't fit this subject may work well with your next subject.

The sense of touch will cover a broad range of feelings. Near the center of the page, name objects you actually were touching.

- Name what you were wearing.
- Tell how your body felt.
  > Which muscles were taut?
  > What was your posture?
  > What were your hands doing?
  > How did your throat feel?
  > How did you hold your mouth? Move your eyes? Breathe?
- Write words descriptive of the atmosphere: the temperature, the source of light and its quality, shadows, the quality of the air. Compare the air to music.
- What was the predominant color in this scene?
- How did you feel about what was happening?
- Name your mood. What was its flavor and color?
- What rhythm describes your feelings?
- Think about the smells in the background of your experience. Name them.

distant tanker

horizons of ocean

waves

waves

floating cap

gulls

paddle

buoy

Chris

tangled rope

jetty

floating life jacket

Robert's hand

cold chest

flotsam

breakers

beach

- How did the objects near you smell?
- How did the people smell? Include yourself.
- What odors were produced by something happening?
- Name wafting scents.

If you had a taste or flavor in your mouth, name it. A young man writing about a diving experience mentioned the salty taste of ocean water in his mouth. Taste may or may not be a part of your remembered experience.

⌒

You can use this technique of brainstorming through your five senses anytime you want to write an account so that it will give a sense of presence to your readers. All you need is a large sheet of paper. Remembering your experience, locate yourself in a certain moment and in a certain place. Then, using your five senses, write words that describe your perceptions. You'll be aware of and use many of them when you begin writing.

The function of language is not to inform but to evoke. What I seek in speech is the response of the other.

JACQUES LACAN
FRENCH PSYCHOANALYST

At this time you have identified an experience to narrate, and now you have a page showing many sensory details that you can include in your account. Refer to this page as you write your account. You probably won't include all the sensations on this page, and you may add other ideas. The brainstorming page just provides a systematic scheme to give you a wealth of specific, vivid material with which to begin writing.

Place your page of ideas where you can see it as you write your rough draft. One good way to begin is "When I was. . . ." This phrase will help you orient readers regarding your age or the stage of your life at the time of the experience. If location is relevant, tell where you were.

Like a news reporter, include when and where and then proceed to tell why and how.

~

Bonnie Gundeloch Johnson wrote the following account by first identifying a significant experience in her life and then, before beginning to write, naming her perceptions at the time. Her description is vivid because she systematically reminded herself of her sensations.

Bonnie is a psychiatric nurse who has worked closely with elderly and dying patients.

Night Trip to Eugene

The experience was part of my awakening. The summer air in hushed sounds rushing past the car under the summer sky. Dark hills to the left, black-and-gray fields in crisscross patterns to the right. My foot on the accelerator, my car traveling the gray strip of highway. Faint sounds trickled from the radio. The dashboard light illuminated the car. My white Australian shepherd dog curled on the seat next to me. I drove on and on from Seattle to Eugene with a two-hour stop in Washougal, Washington, for a stress-filled meeting with my soon-to-be ex-husband about division of the property.

I left at dusk, when the last embers of pink and yellow were fading from the western horizon. Crossing the expansive 205 bridge to Portland, getting gas from an overly cheerful attendant with hair in a dark ponytail down his back. Feeling patronized. Then emerging from the lights of Portland into the dark stretches of open country.

I should stop. I am becoming very tired. I should eat something. I should rest.

Voices in my head. Feeling free. So this is what it is like. Am I free now? Feels free. Feels independent. I feel happy! I should stop. Eyes closing. Oops. Keep eyes open. Very tired. Very tired.

Car ahead, I am rapidly approaching. Foot on brake. Lucky. Darkness. Wake up! Sing. Sing loud! Drive . . . drive. Eyes hurt. Glare. Put on sunglasses. Comfort. Tired. Should stop, should stop. Eyelids closing over parched eyeballs. Open. Please stay open. Open!

So tired. Need to rest just a few seconds. Keep driving. Help. Taillights coming up—slow car. Help! Brake! Lost control. Swerve to left. Hit car. Propelled car off the road. Hit car! Something flipping over in midair. Crashing down. Rolling. Smoking. Rolling. What have I done!

Quiet.

⌐

Slowly read aloud your description. Savor every word. Listen with your eyes half shut as if someone were reading a novel to you. Inhale its vapors.

If you are writing with a gathering of writers, form larger response groups this time because this draft is one you'll especially enjoy hearing. Of course you'll:
* **Suspend judgment.**
* **Size your feet to fit the writer's boots.**
* **Remain mum about what you'll hear.**

Respond by remarking on what, in your own mind, you see, hear, feel, smell, and taste.
   And, if you are acutely curious about something, ask a question.

When you reflect on the draft you've written, take detailed notes in response to the following questions, questions that may cause you to ponder. Your notes are likely to develop into ideas you'll insert into your draft.
* What did the experience you described mean to you?
* Why did you choose to explore this subject at this time?
* How does the experience fit into your life as a whole?
* Within the experience, are there any instances of tenderness? Of grace? Of compassion? Of mercy?

Revise your draft. Expand it. Cross out whatever didn't work as you intended. Change words or phrases. Rearrange paragraphs any way you wish. A well-revised draft is sometimes so covered with marks that it's almost unintelligible.

When your draft sounds right, have it proofread. The amount of proofreading your draft needs depends on your plans for it. If you're going to give copies to only the members of your immediate family and your close friends, then you probably don't need to have it checked for grammar and usage. Your family will like "hearing" you write the way you talk.

If you like to sketch, consider illustrating your final version. Insert any photographs and clippings or documents you may have. Those pictures and other items will be preserved when you make copies of your final version on acid-free paper.

～

If you'd like to try an experiment, use the technique you learned in this chapter on the subject you wrote about for your warm-up writing. Then see how the two rough drafts differ.

The more aware you are of the sensory aspects of your life, the more effectively you can employ the technique described in this chapter. At times when you do rote tasks or when you are inactive, take stock of all sensory perceptions. While sitting in a waiting room, brushing your teeth, watching soccer practice, riding the bus, or raking leaves, systematically ask yourself, "What do I see, hear, smell, feel, and taste?" Observe both close range and distant perceptions. Notice your posture, your breathing, and which of your muscles are tense. Analyze your mood. Not only will you gain skill as a writer, you'll gain appreciation of your own life.

> Eternal One, Sovereign God of the universe: You remove sleep from the eyes, slumber from the eyelids. Help me to be awake this day to the wonders that surround me, alive to beauty and love and aware that all being is precious, that, wherever we go, we walk on holy ground.
> TRADITIONAL JEWISH PRAYER FOR THE MORNING

CHAPTER FIVE

Internalized Places

Religious awe is the same organic thrill which we feel in a forest at
twilight, or in a mountain gorge.

WILLIAM JAMES

AMERICAN PHILOSOPHER AND PSYCHOLOGIST

We carry a landscape within us. The places where we have lived and
worked and felt sharp emotions continue to reside in our being as
part of ourselves. These places can be retrieved through subtle, sensuous
associations that summon an entire scene. Unexpected stimuli—particular
smells; light at a certain slant; a subtle, distant sound; the taste and texture
of a food from our youth—can draw us back in time.

The French author of *Remembrance of Things Past*, Marcel Proust,
reflected on his retrieved memory of a childhood place, brought about
by the flavor of a little cake, a petite madeleine.

> *And suddenly the memory returns. The taste was that of the little
> crumb of madeleine which on Sunday mornings at Combray (because
> on those mornings I did not go out before church time), when I went
> to say good day to her in her bedroom, my aunt Léonie used to give
> me, dipping it first in her own cup of real or of lime-flower tea. . . .
> when from a long-distant past nothing subsists, after the people are
> dead, after the things are broken and scattered, still, alone, more
> fragile, but with more vitality, more unsubstantial, more persistent,
> more faithful, the smell and taste of things remain poised long time,
> like souls, ready to remind us, waiting and hoping for their moment,
> amid the ruins of all the rest; and bear unfaltering, in the tiny
> and almost impalpable drop of their essence, the vast structure of
> recollection.*

It was the smell and taste of the tea-soaked madeleine that retrieved
memories of an old grey house, streets along which he ran errands,

country roads, M. Swann's park, "and the whole of Combray and of its surroundings, taking their proper shapes and growing solid, sprang into being, town and gardens alike, from my cup of tea."

⁓

Our senses both evoke memories in ourselves and, when included in our descriptions, convey a sense of presence. This chapter will guide you in using your senses as you describe a place. You'll apply the technique introduced in chapter four. But first, help your words begin to flow with a quick write.

Rapidly write a description of any place you recall vividly. Your choice of subjects could range from your grandmother's kitchen to a work site, a campsite, or a cathedral; think of any place that has impressed itself on your being. The place may have been nurturing or loathsome. Limit the scope of your description to your visual range from an exact spot.

This quick rough draft will be like a still life taken from the flow of your life. At this time you will set the scene. The description you are developing may turn out to be one you'll develop later by telling about yourself when you were there.

Use any one of the following prompts, or make up your own. Prompts are simply a way to help writers initiate the flow of words. Try any subject that comes to mind, and write rapidly and impulsively. Unplanned writing can be startlingly insightful.

- A place I remember well is . . .
- I could hardly wait to get out of . . .
- I would like to return to . . .

⁓

The following excerpt is from the memoirs of Richard Colley, a cashier at Wal-Mart and a creator of fractal image designs for large latch-hook rugs. He recalls visiting the site in Wilder, Idaho, where the elementary school he attended stood.

The flagpole rose up out of a cement walkway, pointlessly connecting the front steps to the unbusy highway. No longer did Old Glory ruffle its canvas or snap a trusty acknowledgment to the wind. The southward vestige was merely the soft clacking of the flag's chain in the midsummer wind.

Near the northeast corner of the building is a sturdy merry-go-round. I remember making it spin around wildly and then riding it until I was dizzy. My pals and I got it moving around and we played "chicken." The object was to see who could stay on the longest before leaping off. We boys tolerated that play until we were nauseous.

The brick schoolhouse had three levels: basement, ground level, and upper level. Being in fifth-grade was special because townspeople said the building was a "fire trap." The fifth-grade classroom was on the upper level. A window on the west side opened onto the landing of a fire escape. Its special attraction was the long slide that fifth graders could go down during fire drills. The walls of the slide were high with smooth, rounded "arms." The official policy was not to play on the fire escape slide, but many of the more adventurous boys, and occasional tomboys, were wont to break the rule.

This description pictures not only a bleak brick school, but it also shows a place where growing children spun all possible amusement from a merry-go-round and exploited the off-limits thrill of climbing up and whooshing down an outdoor fire escape.

To hear your description if you're writing independently.

- Put your draft aside for a day. Don't read it aloud to yourself until tomorrow. This interim will distance you from it and lend perspective so you can hear it anew.
- Or, ask a close friend to listen to your draft and then tell you what its strengths are, and ask a question about something not told.
- Tape-record your draft, and then listen to it as if it were written by someone else—by someone who is a good friend and whose feelings you respect.

If you're writing with a group of writers, follow the aforementioned guidelines for good listening and respond in the recommended ways.

Should you decide to expand and develop the description you've just written, and you want to give readers a vivid sense of the place, add information about the sensations your five senses consciously or subliminally perceived. We usually describe what we see, but we often forget to use our other senses. Read through your narrative, watching for places where you can add descriptions of:

- Smells
- Sounds
    background sounds
    human sounds
    sounds resulting from actions
- Touch
    the surfaces with which you came into contact
    the way your own body felt
    the atmosphere around you
- Taste

In addition to describing sensory impressions, tell what you felt and thought.

~

Here are remembrances of two different kitchens. The use of sensory descriptions by both writers gives us a feel for each place.

This description is from Rosemary Batori's memoirs. She grew up and lived in England until a handsome American soldier arrived during World War II, courted her, married her, and brought her to his home in Oregon. Notice Rosemary's use of smell.

NORTH WOOTTON FARM, NR. SHERBORNE, DORSET
Breakfast was always served in the enormous, stone-floored kitchen, with Aunt Mae, our stepgrandmother, moving back and forth to the attached dairy room, supervising the dairymaids at their work of separating the milk and churning the butter.

The kitchen opened onto the farm-yard. Any time the door opened, sounds and smells were wafted into the kitchen, the rotting hay, horse and cow manure, an aroma with little appeal to townsfolk but nostalgically attractive to a farmer's granddaughter.

The kitchens of grandmothers seem to be fondly remembered by many memoirists, even though the smells made their noses tickle.

Jean Clark remembers a time when she and her cousin, Roberta, stayed at their Grandmother Robertson's farm for a few days when they were only five and seven years old. Grandmother Robertson taught the girls how to make butter by churning with a broom handle attached to a round wooden dowel.

> *That kitchen was a cozy place. A fire was going in the stove, warming the entire kitchen. Every now and then Grandmother would lift the lid on top of the stove and poke in another stick of wood, at the same time stirring up the fire with a poker, sending a shower of sparks into the air. The smell of sour milk and burning wood tickled our noses. The yeasty aroma of bread rising on top of the warming oven filled the air.*
>
> *Splish! Splash! went the broom handle up and down in the crock. "When will it be done?" we kept asking. Arms were beginning to feel tired. Every now and then Grandmother would stop her bread making or other chores, giving the handle a brisk, firm chug, chug, and offering words of encouragement. "It's almost done."*

Jean used not only the senses of smell, sound, and feeling, but she also included quotations, another effective technique.

〜

You're now ready to write a rough draft for a second description. First gather ideas; on a sheet of notebook paper, name places which you have strong feelings about.

- a safe and happy place in your childhood
- a place where you felt helpless and afraid
- the place where you went to be alone
- your favorite place during your teens
- a place where you learned or discovered something
- a place where something embarrassing happened
- a place where something frightening happened

- a place where you had an encounter with another person
- your first job site
- a place where you felt in jeopardy or threatened
- a place where you were given medical treatment
- your place of worship or meditation or repose
- the location of an important ceremony
- a place you created for yourself and/or your family
- the place where you were when you received bad or good news
- a place where you excelled
- a place where you were defeated
- a place where you were intimate with someone
- the location of a fight
- a place of birth or death
- a restorative place where you felt relaxed and calm

From among your many subjects, pick the place you'd like to write about today. Then store your list of ideas for further descriptions in your greenhouse file.

Use a fresh sheet of paper to prepare to write this description. Following the technique you used in chapter four, write your name in the middle of the page. Imagine that you are in the center of the page and that the paper is the place you are going to describe. Travel mentally to the place you'll describe and locate yourself in a particular spot there.

First, write the names of things you see as you look out from your position. Name things in the foreground and in the background. What colors are they? Be precise. Name exact shades. Include shadows and darkness, as well as the things that stand out.

Next, remember and name the sounds in your place. Think of the natural sounds in addition to sounds made by machinery and by people. Write down sentences spoken by yourself and other people. Include faraway sounds. If the place is quiet, describe its quietness. Someone climbing Mount Audubon above the timberline might hear only the rustle of her own parka blown by the wind, her individual breaths, boots against rock, and the occasional whistle of a marmot.

The sense of touch involves many things: the feel of objects you are touching, the feel of equipment you are using, the feel of your clothing, the way your body feels. Write words descriptive of the textures of things around you. How does the atmosphere feel? The temperature? The humidity? What words describe the mood of the place? What is your own mood?

Taste and smell are interrelated. If something is in your mouth, tell how it tastes, but give more attention to describing smells. Name the nearby odors and then the smells airborne from farther away. Include your own scent as well as that of other people and animals.

⏤

Lilly Burgard describes her feelings about arriving at a reservoir in the Cascade Mountains as the sun was sinking. This is the first paragraph of a chapter entitled "The Reservoir."

> *I looked out the window and the light swirled and shifted, entered my eyes and traveled down my throat, making my solar plexus tingle and burn. "Let's go out in the boat," I suggested. The evening held a unique beauty. It was Indian summer and a full moon was due to rise within the hour. There was a smell in the air, so sweet, I knew the night had potential for magic.*

Lilly takes us beyond the world of physics when she writes, "the light swirled and shifted, entered my eyes and traveled down my throat, making my solar plexus tingle and burn." We know we're in for an interesting boat ride.

⏤

The rough draft you'll now write should be sloppy because it is hurriedly written. Scan your page of notes for ideas, but do not be limited to them. They serve only as a reference for including sensory description as you tell about the place. As you write, allow the feeling of the place to guide you wherever it goes.

Never skip the next step, listening to your draft. Your editing will be far more effective if you've heard your draft read aloud and better yet if you've also heard responses from listeners. Follow the guidelines you've learned for listening and responding.

When you are ready to reflect on this description of a place, jot notes on another sheet of paper in response to the following questions. You may decide to incorporate your reflections into your rough draft.

- Why is the place you chose meaningful to you?
- What does your choice show about your values and about yourself?
- Does the place in some way take you beyond your usual self?
- How would you be different if you had not known this place?
- When do you think of the place, and how do you feel when you remember it?

Look at the notes you've taken and then reread your rough draft. Would integration of your notes into your rough draft give it more depth?

Revise your draft, proofread it, give it a title, and write your final version. If you're writing by hand and make minor errors, just draw neat lines through them and continue. Corrections are not offensive.

It's possible that some descriptions will reflect awe, wonder, reverence, contentment, or joy. Sacredness can occur in improbable places. Equally significant, the absence of those qualities may reveal longing in the soul of the writer.

～

In her writings about her childhood in eastern Oregon during World War II, novelist Debra Burgess-Mohr captures wonderings about hatred and about beauty. Notice that the first paragraph gives the flavor of the historical period, while the second paragraph pinpoints a series of moments in a particular place.

> . . . it seemed that an extraordinary number of young boys, sons of friends of my parents, were called up in the draft, or had enlisted. My mother rolled bandages down at the city hall; my father, who was in the army during World War I, was in some sort of volunteer group that watched the skies at night for enemy planes. Food—sugar, butter, flour, and meat—were rationed; gasoline was allocated ac-

cording to profession. "A" cards went to doctors and farmers, "B" cards were issued to men like my father, and "C" cards were available for the rest.

At night German prisoners of war, who had been brought to our county to work the farms and ranches, worked in the pea cannery in our town. Often, late at night, I awoke to hear them singing in the trucks that brought them into town and transported them back to the barracks behind barbed fences not far from Pendleton. I was amazed at the beauty of their songs and wondered how I could hate someone who made such beautiful music.

CHAPTER SIX

The Soul of a Child

In every child who is born, under no matter what circumstances, and of no matter what parents, the potentiality of the human race is born again; and in him, too, once more, and of each of us, our terrific responsibility towards human life; towards the utmost idea of goodness, of the horror of error, and of God.

JAMES AGEE

AMERICAN JOURNALIST, SOCIAL CRITIC, POET, AND NOVELIST

In writing this chapter you'll give glimpses of a tender part of yourself, your inner life when you were small. You'll show your relationship with members of your family and community, in addition to showing your young self. Begin with a warm-up writing.

Rouse your fluency by first scrawling a quick, careless rough draft. This time, consider writing in response to more than one of the following prompts. You may change the phrasing of any of them, or write about a different subject you remember as important in your childhood.

- My mother (father/other relative) used to always say . . .
- A game I played involved . . . (Tell about the invisible as well as the visible.)
- In my childhood I was most afraid of . . .
- I'm like my (either parent) in these ways . . . and different in these ways . . .
- The person I wanted to be like was . . .
- The way I fit/didn't fit into my family . . .

An especially good way to hear your rough draft is to give it to someone who will read it to you. Sit back and listen to it as if it were written by a stranger. As it is being read, interrupt the reader whenever you want to write notes in the margins as reminders of changes you want to make.

Sara Schwake writes about an unexpected and unwelcome appearance her father made at the elementary school she attended. Notice

> **If you listen to the accounts of fellow writers, remember to remain non-judgmental and confidential about their readings, and respond by first pointing out what you admire about the writing. After that, ask a question.**

how the specific details she gives enable us to picture the father. We see also how Sara felt about him and about herself.

Over the years, Sara has worked as a medical assistant and in clerical support positions; currently, she works for Head Start. She says she "gleans plenty of memoir material" from the tales her two sons tell of their childhood, as well as from her own youth.

> *A time when I did not feel in control was when my father unexpectedly, and without welcome, appeared in the hall outside my third-grade classroom. There he was—all 6' 4" of him, looking as animated as he always could during a manic phase—his wide, goofy smile showing decaying teeth. He didn't care! There he was trying to belong to those traditional wide, shining wooden hallways seemingly filled with young faces staring up at this grinning and gangly man. I would believe that I tried, out of my shock and chagrin, to disappear back into my classroom instead of leaving for a carefree recess. Did my stern, spinster teacher offer me some protection by not letting him know where I was? I couldn't tolerate the link that might be made between me, this growing-into-gangly young girl, and this man who wanted to talk to anyone who'd listen to his often disconnected but constant ramblings. My mom would have been at work and unaware of his likely bored escape and his subsequent foray into a place I had always, until then, felt safe from the havoc he could create. But in truth, I don't remember any other such unwelcome visits. So out there in words I didn't hear, I think an adult sensed how small I felt and shielded me.*

Did you notice that Sara used the adjective "gangly" to describe both her father and herself? Her quick warm-up writing revealed her fear of being associated with her father.

～

Now you are ready to capture ideas for a second subject. On a sheet of paper draw an overview map showing an approximate blueprint of your childhood home or the home in which you spent the most memorable or important part of your childhood. Leave room around the outside walls of the building for the yard or street. Your blueprint does not need to be to scale or even accurate. Distortions and omissions will indicate your perception of your home when you were very young.

In the place where you slept, draw a rectangle for your bed. In the place where you ate, draw an overhead view of the table and chairs. Write the letter *P* where you played indoors. Outside the walls of your house or apartment, indicate trees or shrubs you remember and any outbuildings or other features. Write the letter *P* where you played outdoors.

If you can remember names for the following, write them along the margin of the page:

* the street or road that passed your home
* neighbors
* playmates
* pets or farm animals

Look at your overall blueprint and write a letter *G* where something good happened. Write a letter *B* where something bad happened. Write the letter *T* for "talk" where someone said something that you remember.

Find a partner or a friend who will listen while you explain your blueprint. Point to and tell about everything you've drawn and also about things you haven't drawn. Your account will reach into receded memories, so explain everything you can. Let your blueprint serve as a catalyst for recovering forgotten parts of your childhood.

If you are writing with a partner, listen while she explains her blueprint.

Write a quick, error-strewn draft about any incident you remember from your childhood, or describe a typical event. Think about what you did on weekends. Remember something that happened at school. You could write about an event that was not typical. What special occasion did you eagerly anticipate? Did it turn out the way you expected? You might write about the first time you did something; your first day at school, your first time away from home, the first time you played a sport or were in a performance.

We have romanticized childhood as a time of innocence, and it is. However, ironically, the quality of cruelty resides within the innocent nature of the child. We are first aware of cruelty when we are its victims; we arrive at a higher level of awareness when we recognize ourselves as its perpetrators.

The following excerpt is from the memoirs of Kirsten Jones, an arts consultant and grant writer. Born a first-generation American in San Francisco, she moved to Oregon in search of a more meaningful life.

I remember playing with a gang of neighborhood children only once. I was about nine and probably hadn't lived in that house too long— don't think I even knew the children's names. I must have known them enough to join in, but I have no other memories of them.

Somehow on this particular day, I got to be the leader. How did that happen? We raced up and down the street, shrieking away. As a mob, without any planning or forethought, we started chasing the girl who lived next door to me. I remember the "rush" of being on the attack, of being stronger, of having numbers behind me. We caught her, and she and I had a fight. She pulled my hair really hard, and I pulled hers. I got her down on the ground and sat astride her. In the flush of victory, our eyes locked, and I had no idea what to do next. I began to feel embarrassed, uncomfortable, ashamed. Can't remember what the rest of the gang wanted.

The girl wanted to go home and she promised to come back out after she was cleaned up. Surprisingly, we allowed it and waited. Equally surprising, she came out again, and all awkwardly gathered around and said something—can't remember what. I'm sure that by that time, none of us was happy about how things had turned out. I remember the feeling of respect I had for this girl after she came out and my regret for my actions.

I have no memory of seeing her again. My mother was in bed with a bad back, and my stepfather was overseas. She sold the house soon after, and we moved to Germany.

During my adult life, whenever I've heard of mob actions, I remember that day and how I felt. I remember the feeling of power and I remember the shame. I understand how mobs get out of control—and I've stayed far away.

～

You might again ask someone to read your draft to you so you can listen to it.

If you're writing independently, listen to your own oral reading and then decide what aspect of your writing seems strongest. Ask yourself what questions would occur to a stranger who heard it.

When we hear our early drafts, we often decide to edit them. We may add information, change the way we said something, rearrange paragraphs and sentences, or even cut out parts.

Consider adding sensory description. You may still remember particular smells, tastes, sounds, or the feel of something you touched. It's not necessary to use all five senses; using even a few will render your writing more vivid.

If you remember what someone said, quote that person.

After you've listened to a reading of your rough draft and made the changes your ear told you to make, then reflect on the deeper meanings within your writing. Write sentences or paragraphs in response to the following questions. When you see how you've answered them, you may have thoughts that you'll want to add to your rough draft.

- What was your source of childhood security?
- Whom did you love most?
- What kinds of experience distressed you?
- Were you aware of a child who was "picked on"? If so, what about yourself did your awareness indicate?
- Explain how you do or do not see your childhood as a time of innocence.
- How was harmony created or shattered in your childhood?
- How did you overcome your childhood fears?
- In retrospect, what strengths emerged from within yourself?

When you have revised your rough draft as much as you wish, give it a title, proofread it, and write a final version. Arrange your text on the page around space for photographs of yourself as a child. Be sure to write captions under the pictures. If you enjoy drawing, illustrate this chapter with sketches of your pets, favorite toys, and the places where you played.

⌒

Father Theodore Berktold, an Episcopal rector in Eugene, Oregon, writes about his childhood in Minnesota where his Roman Catholic family lived on a farm. You will see his relationship to his parents and siblings.

My mom would drive into town from our farm on Saturday afternoons and go to confession, dropping some of her nine children off at my grandparents' home one block from the church. I was a quiet and well-behaved child (being older), so I went along with her to church. She always had a baby in her arms. I sat through confession in the pews, and then went into the baptistery with her to light a candle and pray silently. I would get to drop the nickel in the slot of the long brass tube, old and well polished, where the change collected. We would spend what seemed like a long time there (it was probably brief), and she would take me by the hand and carry the youngest child back down the street to my grandparents. We would have a cup of coffee with my grandmother, then drive back to the farm.

Saturday morning was wash day for her, rolling out the washing machine and stands and tubs, heating water in the reservoir of the wood-fired stove, and filling the washing machine with a dipping can. She would wash whites and dress clothes first, ending with muddy clothes (overalls). Saturday supper was always a good meal, because Sunday was a fast day until we had gone to communion. Seated around the table, we would always pray the same words together, hands folded and heads bowed: "Bless us, O Lord, and these thy gifts, we are about to receive from thy bounty, through Christ our Lord, Amen." Saturday evening was a time for us all to take a bath in the same clothes washtubs placed on the floor in front of the wood stove (the oven door open in winter to keep us warm), girls going first (they were cleaner) and boys last, using a bar of homemade soap or lye and tallow. We baked it in a cake pan when we were butchering over Christmas vacation, then cut and stacked it like brownies for later use. After baths, with everyone in pajamas, we would kneel together in the living/dining room and pray the rosary together, pulling chairs out from the table, leaning on the seat and facing the back of the chair. As I got older, I would often lead the rosary. Then we would sit together facing the black-and-white TV on the small table in the corner of the room, Dad would adjust the picture, make popcorn on the wood stove. I would turn the crank to keep a curved wire scraping the bottom of the pot to prevent burned kernels in the hot lard, again produced from our butchering, popping corn we had grown and stored in whole ears under my bed next to the walnuts because my bedroom was above the kitchen and had a dry floor from

the heat of the stove. When Gunsmoke *was over, the TV went off,*
Mom lit a vigil light in front of a picture of Mary, and the older
kids went upstairs to bed; Mary Ann and Peggy to the left, Ted and
Joe to the right, past the toilet mounted in a widened area of the
hallway of the ancient farmhouse. We would all brush our teeth and
get the popcorn shells out, pee, and fall asleep looking at the frost
designs on the window reflected in the brightness of a winter moon.

CHAPTER SEVEN

People Who Etched an Imprint

Whenever two people meet there are really six people present. There is each man as he sees himself, each man as the other person sees him, and each man as he really is.

WILLIAM JAMES

AMERICAN PHILOSOPHER AND PSYCHOLOGIST

The people we remember, beginning with those who tended us when we were very young and continuing up to our present companions and associates, have influenced our assessment of all mankind and of ourselves. Those people are the framework upon which we wove bonds of trust, evolved a sense of self-worth, and learned to work cooperatively and share pleasures. From negative people we learn to be mistrustful and to doubt our own value. This chapter will help you identify key people in your life, write about them and the ways in which they influenced you, and recognize what in yourself responded to them.

~

To find your fluency, scrawl a fast first draft. Make up your own prompt or choose one of the following:

- The person I have felt happiest being with is/was . . .
- Someone who made a period in my life miserable was . . .
- If I could again be with someone from my past, it would be . . . because . . .

After you've written your rough draft, read it to a sensitive listener or a small critiquing group—or read it aloud to yourself. Then take it through the remaining steps of the writing process unless you are now writing with colleagues. If so, set your rough draft aside to complete later.

~

To begin another chapter, first gather ideas. On a sheet of notebook paper, draw rows of oval or square picture frames. Inside each frame you're going to write the name of a person, so make the frames large enough to contain a name. Your gallery of frames may be as simple as circles, or you may draw ornate frames. Toward the end of this chapter, you'll use your gallery in another way, for which you'll need the rows of frames.

Inside the frames, write the names of people who occur to you. It's all right if you list the same name repeatedly, and you may name more than one person in each category. Write the first names that come to mind.

Name someone who has:

- given comfort
- caused distress
- guided you
- befriended you
- elicited desire
- made demands
- received your care
- caused grief
- stifled you
- encouraged you
- sparked fun
- been dependable
- taken care of you
- shaped your beliefs
- raised doubts
- energized you
- stimulated curiosity
- stoked your creativity
- brought out your best
- brought out your worst
- taught you

From your list, choose one person as your subject. The person about whom your feelings, positive or negative, are strongest would be a good choice. After you have chosen your subject, file this list of ideas for future writings in your greenhouse folder.

Write your subject's name in the center of a page. You're going to jot brief notes onto this page that don't have to make sense to anyone but yourself. Your scribblings will revive memories and enable you to include details you might otherwise ignore.

Close your eyes halfway and visualize your subject.

Remember your subject's physical characteristics. Write words that describe the stature, posture, way of walking and moving the body, and any habitual gestures.

Visualize the skin. Imagine touching it. Imagine touching the face. Describe any makeup. How are the teeth?

How would the hair feel? What is its color?

Remember the hands. What is the condition of the nails?

What does the subject wear? What sort of shoes, glasses, jewelry?

How would you describe the voice? Can you remember a typical sentence or phrase? If so, write it down. How did the subject usually breathe?

What smells do you associate with the subject?

Moving from physical characteristics to traits and personality, ask yourself what the subject most enjoyed. What made the person happy? Angry? Weary? Name the person's goals and the worries. What is your subject's predominant mood? What color do you associate with your subject?

If you were going to liken your subject to an animal, which animal would you choose? If to weather, what sort of weather? If to music, what category of music? If to a vehicle, what kind of vehicle? What type of plant does your subject suggest? A cactus? A vine?

You now have more notes than you're likely to use, but you have brought to mind many observations you can use as you describe your subject. The following prompts are ways of beginning this draft:

- Someone who . . .
- I will never forget . . .

Scrawl a messy first draft.

If you cannot get rid of the family skeleton, you may as well make it dance.

GEORGE BERNARD SHAW

IRISH PLAYWRIGHT, CRITIC, AND NOVELIST

The following description by Lowell Andrew Thomas is set in Mississippi, where he spent his early life. He and his wife, Peggy, now live in Oregon.

Someone who meant a lot to me was my Granny. When I was born, she was seventy-three and had failing eyesight that eventually left her blind. Some memories:

- *That she was stooped and skinny with dark Cherokee skin and didn't talk much except to me.*
- *Drying watermelon seeds and putting them into little cotton bags with drawstrings while listening to Granny tell me how they would turn into watermelons again after we planted them in the spring.*
- *Sitting before the fireplace in a room with unpainted wooden walls that were lit by kerosene lamps.*
- *Getting off the school bus one day and being attacked by a guinea that had her nest in the roadside ditch. As I ran across the yard screaming, the guinea on top of my head clawing my scalp, I saw my Granny run from the house and sprint across the yard with her homemade broom. I was so surprised to see that she could run that I almost forgot my pain and terror.*
- *How carefully she kept her yard swept and how refreshing it felt to lie upon the naked earth on a hot day.*
- *After my family moved to town, going to the store on my bicycle to buy snuff for my Granny. She liked Levi Garrett. It came in little cans, and the plain flavor had a white label and the Scotch flavor had an orange label. Each came with a flat wooden spoon for dipping.*
- *Granny sitting in her chair the last few years of her life rocking back and forth slowly all day long.*
- *How her room during those years was in back of the house, away from the rest of the family.*

• Listening to my Granny tell about being an orphan who was taken in by a family named Grey and how the Greys often had company for days at a time and held dances at their house.

• How I had a fight with Granny one day and said mean things and how shocked and sorry I was when she cried like a little girl.

• Running in from playing one day to find my Granny sitting on the floor in the back of the long dark hallway. I nearly laughed to see her there until she called to me in pain from a broken hip.

• Going to her funeral and not crying and being praised by my father for acting like a man.

• That she said she loved me more than she had ever loved anyone or anything.

～

To revise this draft, make any changes you wish. Freely insert additional information.

Check to see if you described your subject's appearance and personality and told how that person affected you.

～

In this excerpt from her memoirs, Adrienne Lannom shows how her grandmother affected her.

I don't remember that she ever said to me, "I love you." It sort of came out of her like waves washing over me. Now that I've just written that, I recognize the pull the ocean has for me—the sense of homecoming, the laying down of cares and burdens, the long ecstatic intake of breath and the ocean smell filling me.

Grandma had a special smell that was unlike any other that I've experienced before or since my first and last memories of her. I think it was a combination of baking and cooking smells, especially bread-making smells, and the smell of a lotion she ritually applied every night after she unpinned and brushed her hair. She wasn't a Norman Rockwell picture-book grandmother, although she was tiny and round and sturdy. The bread she took from the oven often failed to rise, sat heavily on the table, and tasted deliciously of failed yeast. It was an outward and visible sign of her love and was always there for me when I came to visit.

Grandma never instructed or corrected. There was nothing I did that went unaffirmed. I was wonderful in her sight, and everything I did was also—being a crepe-paper jonquil in a nursery school pageant, playing in my first piano recital, winning a third-grade spelling bee, introducing her to my first real boyfriend, running up the four half-flights of stairs to her apartment after she pressed the buzzer that let me push open the heavy downstairs door, and hugging her.

And I knew myself to be a different person with her—a better person. For her, I wanted to be perfect, doing all the things my parents struggled in vain to get me to do at home. So it was that after I became a parent and my children grew up and went away, I couldn't wait to become a grandparent. I thought they'd never get married, and then I wondered if they'd ever have children. I should have trusted that love like Grandma's couldn't be denied and that it goes on through me to each one of my grandchildren and will, through them, to theirs.

⌐

Consider whether your subject embodies any of the following qualities or stimulates them in yourself:

- generosity
- devotion
- mercy
- compassion

If you can remember the words someone spoke, even approximately, put quotation marks around them and include them in your narration. Include your own spoken responses in the same way. Dialogue gives a sense of drama and immediacy to writing. Imagine what the last novel you read would be like without dialogue.

Enjoy revising this draft.

You may have written a gift. If you wrote about someone you admire or love, consider making a copy of your description to give to that person. A workshop participant who wrote about her deceased sister could not give her writing to her sister, so she made copies for her sister's children. As Thanksgiving approached, she mailed the copies to her nieces and nephews as a celebration and offering of thanks for their mother.

A young man who had written an admiring description of his hard-working, single mother gave it to her on her birthday; the next time his writing class met, he reported to classmates that she cried when she read it. An attractive way to present your description as a gift is to roll it like a scroll and tie a ribbon around it. A red ribbon around your scroll makes a memorable valentine present.

> For love is an attitude toward reality—usually of someone finite toward something infinite.
>
> JOSEPH BRODSKY
>
> U.S. POET LAUREATE, 1991–1992

If you are imaginative, experiment using the following suggestion. Take your gallery of "portraits" from your greenhouse folder. Squint at the picture frames and mentally transpose them into mirror frames. Then in each mirror, "see" what quality in yourself was evoked by the person whose name lies behind the reflection. Look at yourself in relation to the person. What about yourself caused you to respond as you did to the person?

Make notes on your observations about yourself as you move from mirror to mirror. You may gain surprising insights. If thoughts from these observations are appropriate to add to the descriptions you just wrote, slip them in. If you gained an insight that would be a subject for yet another chapter, mark it with a giant asterisk as a reminder for future writing.

Proofread your revised rough draft, and write a final version on acid-free paper.

CHAPTER EIGHT

Adolescent Angst

How did I get here? Somebody pushed me. Somebody must have set me off in this direction and clusters of other hands must have touched themselves to the controls at various times, for I would not have picked this way for the world.

JOSEPH HELLER
AMERICAN NOVELIST

Adolescence is a time of daring hopes, bolts of joy, undeserved despair, self-doubt, arrogant egoism, rudeness, and painful sensitivity. It's frequently a time when faith in the teachings of our parents ruptures, and we flounder among peers. We experiment, take risks, weep in secret, defile our bodies, and pray.

Remembering your adolescence is likely to be both amusing and painful. You may find that unbearable embarrassments have now become bearable and insurmountable problems have been surmounted, but don't be surprised if some memories still cause you to cringe. Think back on the times of elation, as well as on the awkward occasions. Perhaps your adolescent soul was in a time of molting. Regard it gently now.

~

Write a quick, careless draft to one of the following prompts, or tell about a happening you remember vividly. To rev up your writing, begin with one or more of these prompts:

- The most fun I had in high school was . . .
- I felt humiliated when . . .
- My big goal was to . . .
- Mother (Dad/other) was probably right, but I still wish . . .
- Mother (Dad/other) was wrong, and I wish . . .
- A time when I disappointed myself . . .

- I felt different because . . .
- I was scared when . . .

⁓

David M. Seligson has devoted most of his adult life to the welfare of children. Even when he worked as a public relations director for the Portland Trail Blazers, he was creating programs for young people. In this part of his memoirs, he remembers his adolescence.

> *I look at my father, in his big easy chair made of plastic leather cracked by time, unaware I was struggling with how to reach him. I asked him often enough to get out of the glass booth that I imagine surrounded him. My voice at first impenetrable and then it became silent for I only talked to myself.*
>
> *Yet I loved him. He was kind, wouldn't yell, he just damn never talked to me about anything. I often smelled his cherry pipe tobacco when he wasn't there. I would pick up the leaves and roll them between my two fingers and put his pipe, unlit, in my mouth to be closer to him and I was, but the boyhood despair I masked and became a nice quiet kid who went around to the new suburban house and ripped out plumbing like it was cotton candy. I was angry and I couldn't tell him nor could I tell him I loved him.*

⁓

Read your rough draft aloud to a trusted friend or to yourself.

When listeners in your response group ask questions about your account, make notes of their questions. We tend to feel that we've taken care of the missing information when we answer orally, and we forget to amend the writing. Later, when you revise this rough draft, you'll see your notes and remember the questions. Then you can decide whether or not to insert the requested information into your final draft.

You're ready to gather ideas for your second writing. On a new page draw a large stick figure that represents yourself when you were an adolescent.

On your figure's round head, draw hair styled the way you wore your hair in high school. Near the margin of your paper at head level, name the items you used to style your hair.

Dress your figure in the type of shirt or blouse or sweater you used to wear.

Draw pants or a skirt the shape and length you wore. If brand names were important, write them down. Indicate pockets and their contents. To the side, draw the sort of notebook or backpack or other equipment you toted.

Shoe your figure with the type of footwear you wore. Draw socks or stockings if they were visible.

If you wore them, add jewelry, your watch, braces, body ornaments, electronic items, and any other paraphernalia you carried with you.

Along the margin of your page list:
- sports you played
- a musical instrument you played
- your favorite class
- your favorite teacher
- your worst class and teacher
- the name of your best friend
- an enemy
- someone you emulated
- after-school activities you joined
- jobs you had
- what you did on Saturdays
- titles of popular songs
- a book you reread
- a movie you remember
- a TV show you watched
- issues you argued about with a parent
- something you did that was dangerous or risky
- the ways you felt inadequate
- your appraisal of your body
- your worries

Though your stick figure is only two-dimensional, it, with your lists,

Thought I was adopted

football
basketball
running after girls
Mr. Crowley
civics + government
Mr. Shock, physics
Hammy
Stevo

zits

bagged groceries

sneaking into drive-in movie

white t-shirt

Basketball

I wanna Hold Your Hand
lovie, lovie

hit speed of 110 mph
swimming at the quarry

volume of records
S+W

← levi's

3 - white socks

← converse all stars

has brought you in touch with your adolescent years. You'll now be able to recollect emotions you felt at that time. If you are writing with a fellow writer, take time to explain your drawing and lists to each other; your explanations will bring back still more memories.

Write about a happening that was important to you when you were an adolescent. Even though an experience that made an impact on you might not have appeared important to the people around you, it could have shaped your feelings about yourself or a decision you made that affected the next years of your life. To identify subjects, think back on triumphs and failures, discoveries, lessons learned, or even the giddiness or dismay of a first date.

Your account is likely to reflect your social relationships, a primary concern for most adolescents. It may show how you wanted to be seen by others. Make notes about who your friends were and what it was about them that attracted you. What about you attracted them? Which adults did you attempt to impress? What did you learn about work and about play? How did your peers and mentors help you—or lead you astray?

Your writing will be most vivid if you choose a particular incident and then imagine yourself in the location where it happened.

Use your five senses as you prepare to write your account. From a particular spot in the scene you describe, name what you see, hear, feel, smell, and taste.

Describe the people. Quote what they said and what you said. Tell what happened. Reveal your feelings at that time.

> There came a time when the risk to remain tight in the bud was more painful than the risk it took to blossom.
>
> ANAÏS NIN
> FRENCH WRITER

The next step is to experience this draft aurally. In the same way you would be kind to a stranger or polite to an alien, regard the teenage person you once were with forbearance. If your oral reading sounds like a confession, so be it. We have all been adolescents.

You know the guidelines for good listening and for responding to rough drafts. Apply them as you hear this draft.

～

Alan Reeder has been a singer, songwriter, and teacher of handicapped children. At three universities he directed programs for teachers of handicapped students, and he now lives and writes in southern France for part of each year. This paragraph is lifted from a section of his memoirs about his adolescence. Notice Alan's effective integration of vocabulary from his rebellious youth.

> *The rebel in me was expressed in other ways—a long pompadour hairdo, you know the kind I mean; self-inflicted initials carved into my wrist with a razor blade, a silver chain and medallion hung welded around my neck, removable only if you removed my head. That was the idea. There were hands taped on a Friday night, ready to fight the perfect stranger. "Midnight auto" excursions were a source of excitement and a way to show off. Yes, the "caper" for those who know about such things.*

～

Reflect on your rough draft by writing answers to the following questions. You may be able to expand one or more of your answers into significant, additional material for your memoirs.

- How did you fit or not fit into your family? Into your class at school?
- What were your aspirations?
- What were your fantasies?
- What caused you to feel guilty?
- What does this show about about the values of your family? About your own values?
- What was your greatest fear?
- To what extent did religious faith play a part in your adolescence?
- For whom or what did you feel empathy or compassion?
- In what ways did you help someone or play a supportive role?

- In what ways were you helped?
- What was your source of hope?

⌐

The year she was a sophomore in her Palo Alto high school, Liane Cordes was inspired by her English teacher, Ms. Fletcher, to become an English teacher herself, an aspiration Liane fulfilled.

Ms. Fletcher stood tall and straight behind the lectern, reading the attendance sheet in a deep, sexy voice. She didn't look like any English teacher I'd ever had.

She was dressed in a simple yet elegant gray straight skirt, matching sweater, white blouse with a red ribbon tie at the collared neck, black heels and stockings. Huge red earrings swayed as her head looked up to greet each person whose name she read. She smiled the deep red, lipstick smile at each one of us. When she got to my name, she hesitated a moment, and I waited for her to massacre it. Almost every teacher who'd ever had my brother made a mess of my last name. And no one could pronounce my first name. Ms. Fletcher was brand new to the school, so I waited for her to botch it.

"LIE ANNE CORDS." Even her botching my name sounded sexy. Susie Prichette giggled two rows over, and Judy Burrell smiled.

Ms. Fletcher asked if she had pronounced it right. I raised my hand. "Here," I said. "My name is Leeann."

Ms. Fletcher smiled at me, a larger, more welcoming smile than she'd given anyone up to that point. She never lost her dignity even amidst the snickering.

"Let me make a note of that. That is an unusual spelling. Did I get your last name OK?"

My gosh, I thought, this lady cares who I am.

"No, ma'am," I replied. "Cordes. It's Liane Cordes. You know, like tortoise. My softball team's called Cordes's Tortoises, if that helps you remember."

She laughed deep and long, her dark brown eyebrow arching playfully above her right eye. "Ah, that's a perfect way to remember it. Thank you," she winked at me and went on.

From that moment on, I sat in the front row of that sophomore English class and vowed I'd be just like her, a sexy, deep-voiced English teacher who made it a point to know and value each student. I'd dress with class and color, and I'd command respect like her by standing tall and dignified no matter what happened. And I'd be passionate about English, mostly about literature and writers. I'd read passages from The Red Badge of Courage *with drama, with heart. I'd make the words sing off the page until every kid who heard Stephen Crane's words would never want to fight or go to war. They'd all want to be English teachers, gentle and compassionate and pronouncing every student's name exactly and with great care.*

～

Based on listeners' suggestions, your reflections, and most of all your own intuition, revise your rough draft.

Consider having your rough draft proofread if you plan to distribute it widely or if you would feel more comfortable with a corrected final draft.

I think somehow, we learn who we really are and then live with that decision.

ELEANOR ROOSEVELT

AMERICAN POLITICAL LEADER, U.S. DELEGATE TO THE U.N.

Some people who have used the prompts in this book have enthusiastically written rough drafts without taking time to write final versions as they advanced from chapter to chapter; that is a good thing to do if one's purpose is to explore the interior life without creating a lasting book. However, some of those people did intend to produce books. Eventually, as the rough drafts accumulated, the task of writing many final versions grew large.

If this situation could happen to you, resolve now to write final versions as you proceed. They don't have to be perfect. When you make mistakes, just cross them out. If your final version is somewhat sloppy, your readers will recognize that you, like all of us, are a busy person, not a professional book publisher.

CHAPTER NINE

Events That Shape the Course of Your Life

Life is like a game of cards. The hand that is dealt you represents determinism; the way you play it is free will.

JAWAHARLAL NEHRU

INDIA'S FIRST PRIME MINISTER

We are able to control some aspects of our lives, but events and circumstances often elude our control. Employment opportunities, the economy, opportunities for education, our own health, even crop failures can alter our plans. The interweaving of our wills with chance, or destiny, reveals much about us. As you write this chapter, you'll show how events shaped your life and how you shaped events.

First, write a quick, messy, twenty-minute draft beginning with one of the following prompts:
- A time when I did not feel in control was when . . .
- I had to make the best of it when . . .
- I realized my life would be different when . . .

This rough draft may be about feelings you have never before expressed, even to close friends. You might wait until tomorrow to read

> You may have confided about a time of difficulty or major change, a soul-searching time. If so, this story could be less easy to read to listeners than past drafts have been. Form small response groups, and remember that listeners must not judge the writer's actions or feelings nor tell outsiders about what was read.
>
> Respond to each other's rough drafts by first pointing out an admirable aspect of the writing and then asking a question for further information.

it aloud to yourself. A passage of time between the writing and the hearing will engender perspective.

When you read your story, listen to it in the same way a caring friend would listen.

This is an excerpt from "Family Memories" by Thelma Merrick Hicks. Her parents homesteaded in the panhandle of west Texas where she was the eldest of nine children. Her memoirs show how weather can affect the course of one's life.

> *The drouth of 1917 was the beginning of a disastrous period. With no rain, the sand and wind swept the pastures clean of vegetation: Grass roots stood above the ground like coarse spider webs, the fields lay bare, the livestock walked the fences reaching for a bite of greenery. And now came the fearful news that the United States had entered World War I. It was June 5, 1917. Induction centers were opened and the young men had to sign up for the war.*

~

In preparation for your second writing, list dates for about a dozen events or circumstances that shaped your life. You will probably think first of occasions such as marriages, moves, career beginnings, discoveries of interests, births, and new contacts. Also include events that altered your life such as changes in health, inheritance of money, failures, and wars or natural disasters.

Alongside each date, name what happened. If you don't remember the year, an estimate will suffice. Name events as they occur to you; your list need not be chronological.

If you're writing independently, imagine telling a good friend about one of the experiences.

If you're writing with other people; find a partner.

Tell your partner what happened on any of the listed dates. Go into detail. Tell how your life was affected. Tell how you felt.

Listen while your partner relates a happening in his or her life. Help that person consider the impact of the event on subsequent experiences. Ask how your partner was emotionally affected.

Pivotal Experiences

Year	Event
'53	move to Colorado
'59	death of Norris
'62	admission to Michigan State
'68	job in California
'70	marriage
'82	Mom's death
'73	birth of twins
'78	divorce
'79	religious conversion
'83	remarriage
'92	joining outdoor league
'99	starting the new business

Choose any of the experiences from your list to write about now. It may be the one you related to a listener, or it may be a different subject. Sometimes talking about what we plan to write carries us on to another subject that seems to edge in, demanding, "Write about me first!" As usual, be guided by your inclination. You'll write best when you write about the topic that fuels your enthusiasm. Think of your list as a catalyst that leads to more subjects; don't be limited to the list.

The list you made is a rich source of ideas for further chapters in your memoirs, so place it in your greenhouse file for future reference.

Write a rough draft, proceeding carelessly, freely, and impulsively, knowing that rough drafts can be changed radically. Tell not only what happened but also how your life was affected and how you felt about it.

～

The following excerpt, set in 1932 when she was nine years old, is from the memoirs of Betty Jean Speck. She says of herself, "I write because no other medium can give such pleasure, such depth of soul and so many lifelong friends as does creating one's diaries, journals, letters, essays, poems, or prose."

Notice that Betty's memoirs are written in the present tense, an option that sometimes helps writers convey a strong sense of surroundings and immediacy. If the drafts you've been writing seem cursory, try using the present tense.

> *It's clear and cold our early December morning in Wallace, Idaho. A pale sun barely visible over the eastern mountain casts no spell of warmth. The rectangular wood and metal–reinforced trailer Daddy built now bulges and towers, laden with Mother's canned goods. It's covered with Daddy's ten-man hunting tent and strapped down with heavy rope just like he hitches loads on pack animals. This load won't budge an inch no matter how far we travel!*
>
> *Mother slowly closes and locks the front door, comes down the wood steps, then the cement steps to the street. She hands Lydia Tabor our keys since Lydia will rent out our little house until this depression is over when it might then sell. They hug one another, promising to "write often." We bid farewell to our other neighbors gathered to see us off—tears sting as I give bear hugs to my best girlfriend, Jean Tabor, my pals Habut, Vernon, and Roy Carlson, and to the grown-ups. Already this morning I have walked, touched, and blown kisses to the Indian Path up our mountain that spells "big adventure," to*

our vacant lot where Daddy sets up my play tent every summer, to our lilac tree of fragrant spring bouquets for Mother and then lazy summer shade for childhood daydreaming, then to each room in our house, including down steep wood stairs to my best spot of all—our cellar.

In 1932, I'm nine years old, have just started the fifth grade and am in love with my teacher, Miss Alma Schilling. I'm as scared as I am sad—this seems the end of my happy childhood days as I listen to worries about thousands of dust bowl refugees flooding California. Will our food supply last until Daddy can find a job? Will we be able to pay rent for a decent place to live? Added to that I whimper, "Don't they really have any mountains? Does it snow just once in a while, maybe?"

Our new 1932 Chevy sedan begins slowly to move down Queen Street. The windows reveal an interior packed almost to the roof with bedding, linens, and clothes. I am packed on top of pillows at one side of the backseat. Clutching my doll, I wonder teary-eyed what child now has my most treasured of all toys—my dear little G.E. electric range that I could not bring. As we turn the corner I wave— my friends' faces are blurred images to treasure. Daddy and Mother drew from savings for our new car for this long journey and unknown future. Daddy will do all the driving, and Mother will hold Teddy on her lap all the way to California.

⌒

Following the guidelines for good listening and responding, listen to an oral reading of your rough draft. If you also listen to the writing of a partner or fellow writers, you may feel moved by sympathetic feelings. Listen to your reading of your own draft with sympathy, and learn everything you can from all the readings you hear.

To reflect on the spiritual dimensions of your account, write responses to the following questions. Reflection through writing leads to discoveries we would not otherwise make.

- Was the experience transformational, and if so, how? Did you discover new opportunities for yourself?

- What inner qualities are reflected by your response to the experience?
- What was the source of your strength, resilience, courage, and enthusiasm?
- Tell about any ways in which your response to the event expanded your intellect or talents.

⁓

Laura Lyford is a medical secretary by trade and an aspiring writer. In this part of her memoirs she describes the beauty of her house and then tells why she had to leave it.

> . . . *My husband had gone insane, and nothing I had tried to do seemed to help him in any way. I had brought my babies home to this house, watched the sun rise on so many mornings, scrubbed every corner, cooked thousands of meals there—but I had to leave. Where would I go? What would I do? I had no answer, only an urgent call that said: Get out! Save yourself!*
>
> *I packed up a few changes of clothes, loaded them in the car, and drove into town. I thought I'd go to a laundromat but I ended up at the Dairy Mart, checking a phone book for motels. I never imagined I would be starting out on my own at the age of forty-five, but I did it.*

⁓

Revise the content of your drafts in any way you wish. Add or delete material, and change or rearrange it. Then give this chapter a title.

Look for documents to embellish this entry. In albums or scrapbooks or boxes of saved items, you may be able to find:

- certificates
- conscription papers
- employment contracts
- deeds
- newspaper accounts
- announcements
- letters

- diary entries
- other records or documents

Decide where you'll insert the document, and indicate space for it on your rough draft. When you write your final version, you'll leave room to place it where you want it. If you don't care to include documents, that's OK, too.

Handwrite, type, or keyboard your final draft onto acid-free paper.

This would be a good time to begin carrying a portable notebook. Find a lightweight notebook that you can carry everywhere you go, a book to stash in the car or tote in your bag or pack. Cheap spiral notebooks work well.

Copy ideas for future chapters onto the first pages, and write drafts on the following pages. As you generate ideas for each chapter in *Memoirs of the Soul,* you will list many subjects from which you'll write only two drafts. If you write the other ideas in the front of your portable notebook, then wherever you are—in a waiting room, at the laundromat, on a commuter train, any place where you find yourself with a few minutes of free time—you can make progress in writing your memoirs.

CHAPTER TEN

Struggles and Satisfactions

I went to the woods because I wished to live deliberately, to front only the essential facts of life, and see if I could not learn what it had to teach, and not, when I came to die, discover that I had not lived. I did not wish to live what was not life, living is so dear; nor did I wish to practice resignation, unless it was quite necessary. I wanted to live deep and suck out all the marrow of life, to live so sturdily and Spartan-like as to put to rout all that was not life, to cut a broad swath and shave close, to drive life into a corner, and reduce it to its lowest terms, and, if it proved to be mean, why then to get the whole and genuine meanness of it, and publish its meanness to the world; or if it were sublime, to know it by experience, and be able to give a true account of it in my next excursion.

HENRY DAVID THOREAU

AMERICAN WRITER, TEACHER, ORATOR, GARDENER, PENCIL-MAKER,

SURVEYOR

The efforts we make when we undertake any endeavor reflect our sympathies and enthusiasms. Whether we succeed or fail, our initiative is an essential component of ourselves. In particular, our strivings to surmount obstacles reveals our strengths, our beliefs and values, our capability, and our courage. This chapter will guide you in writing about times when you made a determined effort.

You'll also write about satisfaction you've enjoyed. You'll first bring to mind the activities you find satisfying and then show how you savor at least one of them. Contentment is as much a part of our essential being as is effort.

～

Today, as you prepare to write, take a few minutes to review the steps of the writing process. Turn back to chapter two to remind yourself of the procedure you're following. In most of the upcoming chapters, the steps of the writing process will not be explicitly stated, but you'll follow them as a matter of course.

To assemble a choice of ideas for your writing, name the activities that have given you pleasure as a young person and as an adult. These activities might range from playing ball to sewing, from painting to swimming, from constructing a house or repairing the car to caring for a child. Name things you've done with a partner or group of people, as well as by yourself.

Write "Enjoyable Activities" as the heading for a list. Identify activities that have involved:

- making something
- using your brain
- using equipment
- using your body

Also, identify:

- activities you do by yourself
- activities you do with a partner
- activities you do at home and away from home
- activities you do in a group

Write a quick description of yourself doing something that gives you pleasure. Satisfying experiences are sometimes sensory; if yours is, think of how you can include your five senses in this description. Show your satisfaction through your actions and possibly through dialogue.

Possible prompts are:

- When I was young I loved to . . .
- An activity that has given me pleasure . . .
- Whenever I have time to do what I enjoy, I . . .
- An experience that makes me feel good is . . .

⌒

The selection on page 83 is by Lilly Burgard, who has loved telling stories since she was a child. She now finds the writing of stories yet more magical and says her memoirs, telling the story of her choice to

Enjoyable Activities

making things
— making wine
— herb box
— photo album

using head
— programming computer
— class at City college
— reading
— crossword puzzles

daytime
— lunch at cafe
— stopping at museum
— walking through park

evening
— movies
— reading
— visiting with friends

equipment
— camera
— computer
— kitchen appliances

body
— jogging
— tennis
— yoga

by myself
— reading
— walks
— sauna

partner
— eating
— concerts +
  movies
— sex

be a single mother, will create a link between her childhood and that of her young son.

I have always enjoyed cooking, watching others cook, helping others cook, cooking for others, as well as prepping the food and not cooking it. Like the time I worked in a tremendously busy delicatessen in Ann Arbor, I never tired of cooking. It is a love.

When I was in college, I would cook a special meal every Friday night, with no guests invited. Yet, every Friday someone would drop by unexpected and I would offer a warm, luscious feast. Soon I found the apartment full of unexpected guests every Friday night. Years later I met my match. Dave amazed me. Even before he moved into our communal household he spoke of cooking in a way that resonated in my heart. The first day he arrived he made a pile of fresh pasta and had it draped over chairs and laundry stands throughout the house while he cooked huge batches of pasta sauce to can.

I had never met anyone with this kind of attitude toward food before. We spoke the same language of texture, color, and smell; the fine art of peeling garlic and drooling came easily. He loved to joke and to laugh, but he was always serious about food, even in his gaiety.

"Pancakes are my specialty," I said. He said that his were better. So we had a pancake bake-off. One Sunday I served. I made a huge batch, but only Dave partook of the event. It was true, they were unbelievably good. They almost made him cry. "What is the secret ingredient?" he asked after guessing everything but the mystery item. "I have to know!"

"Pecan meal!" I exclaimed triumphantly.

The next Sunday was his turn to serve. He invited lots of guests for the event. The kitchen was completely taken over by him two hours prior to the gathering. The excitement and energy in the house thrilled and warmed me. It is a feeling I have come to associate with Home, with a capital H.

The guests arrived and all were fit in a most comfortable manner around the table that should only fit four. The food was amazing and the warmth encircled us all with a gentle hum. Dave won, hands down. I have yet to be able to accomplish this art of Home that he illustrated to me so wonderfully.

Lilly's memoirs describe her wanderings in India and southeast Asia, her search for a philosophy and for enlightenment. In contrast to her travel writings, this particular entry shows her desire to create a strong sense of home.

～

If you're writing independently, read your draft aloud to an imaginary friend.

Something new: Guess Who the Author Is. If you're writing with a group of writers, you'll enjoy redistributing your rough drafts so listeners won't know who wrote them. Read aloud the draft handed to you, and ask the group to guess who wrote it. Not only is this guessing game great fun, but you'll become more aware of individual writing styles, points of view, and assumptions. You'll see what about your own writing is identifiable to other writers.

To assemble ideas for a second composition, make lists of the advantages you've enjoyed and obstacles you've faced. Form two columns. Give one column the heading "Advantages" and the other column the heading "Obstacles."

The following categories may help you think of personal advantages and disadvantages: physical, mental, educational, economic, familial, circumstantial, historical, accidental, and spiritual.

Some of your listings might appear on both columns.

Choose an adversity or hardship about which to write. It may be something you've overcome or something impossible to surmount. By writing about an adversity, you'll reveal hopes, aspirations, strivings, concerns, and emotions that are unlikely to emerge if you were to write about the advantages you've enjoyed.

At a later time, after you've written about an obstacle, write about an advantage.

Write your rough draft impulsively and rapidly so that unplanned words can emerge. Sometimes we're surprised by what we write. Subconscious understandings and wisdom can appear and astound us. Later when we revise the rough draft, we can decide whether to retain or discard any unexpected thoughts.

Describe not only what happened but also how you felt about the experience. What emotions did you feel? Were you guided by them, or did you squelch them? Readers won't know you unless you show your feelings. A workshop participant who had worked for the Red Cross in stricken places throughout the world wrote about events that had happened and the noble work she had done, but she forgot to share her feelings and thoughts. Her chapters read like dry reports. A technique that eventually enabled her to bring her emotions into her writing was to imagine herself on location and to write in the present tense to describe what she could see, hear, feel, smell, and taste. She added information about her emotions and quotations that expressed her thoughts. By using these techniques, she succeeded in showing not only what she had experienced but also the caring, courageous person she was.

> I think that in order to write really well and convincingly, one must be somewhat poisoned by emotion, dislike, displeasure, resentment, fault-finding, imagination, passionate remonstrance, a sense of injustice—they all make fine fuel.
>
> EDNA FERBER
> AMERICAN NOVELIST AND PLAYWRIGHT

Read your rough draft to a loving listener, or read it aloud to yourself.

⌒

The following excerpt from an autobiography by Bruce Novak will be published in *Facing the Shadow in Education: Discovering Its Magical, Transformative Power,* edited by Regina Foehr. Bruce is a doctoral student at the University of Chicago where he helps prepare high school English teachers.

When I entered the sixth grade, I thought I was pretty much the perfect student. . . .
What did it mean to be "the perfect student"? My grades, of course, were quite high in every "important" subject. (I had a deathly fear of, and hence developed almost no abilities in, the two "unimportant"

*subjects of art and physical education, but no one thought it worth the
bother to offer me any significant help in overcoming these fears, because
these subjects were seen to be so peripheral.) From a very young age, I
learned to live for my grades, to identify myself with the grades I earned,
to see the set of numbers that arrived every nine weeks on a small, pale
blue card as a revelation of my true worth, in numerical terms.*

～

*My first prominent memory from sixth grade is from the perform-
ance of a skit a group of us had been asked to write. Our assignment
was to dramatically portray as many of the fascinating aspects as we
could of the Canadian province of Newfoundland. I remember nothing of the skit now and very little about Newfoundland. What I
do remember is that we made a bridge between the two parts of
Newfoundland by staging a boat trip between the populous island
territory of Newfoundland proper and the territory of Labrador on
the mainland. To liven this up, and to provide our audience with
firsthand experience of the plenteous aquatic population that provided
the main livelihood of our province, we had our boat crash and sink,
forcing us to swim to shore amid a huge school of codfish.*

*I thrashed wildly on the tile floor, letting loose a feeling of primitive
physical joy that as a determined nonathlete I had never had the
opportunity to feel before. Perhaps it won't be easy for you to see this,
but that physical feeling represented a huge emotional release for me.
For the previous five years, I had acted as if I did not have a body,
as if all that I was was a mind. In real life, I refused to go swimming,
except under the duress of the requirements of summer camp. The
feeling of my arms, legs, and stomach thrashing against the cold tiles,
which I pretended were codfish, was thus a dramatic moment of
liberation for me. I was portraying the desperation of a man trying
to save his life by swimming through icy, choppy, fishy waters. What
I felt inside, though, was the sudden sense of a life—of personal,
incarnated flesh rather than disembodied, depersonalized mind—
that was worth saving, a life that suddenly mattered.*

Notice that as Bruce reached the part of this narrative where he broke the restraints of his earlier identity, he chose the strong nouns *joy, release, duress, liberation, desperation,* and the vivid verb *thrash.*

~

At your leisure, consider the spiritual dimensions of your rough drafts. Take notes as you name:
- the people who inspired or encouraged you
- the capabilities you have shown
- instances of your creativity or courage
- an example of your resolution
- talents you have
- other strengths you possess
- the source of your patience
- the source of your energy

You will observe that most of the questions for reflection expose your good qualities and lead you to seek their sources. This book will bring to light parts of yourself you may not have fully appreciated. Most introspective people are already well aware of their shortcomings and do not benefit from further reflection on them. Granted that at certain times, such as during psychoanalysis, we do need to pursue the causes of our discomfort; however, the goal of such analysis is usually different from your purposes at this time. Though you will write about disappointments in your life and in yourself as you use this book, the insights emerging from your reflections will direct your voyage toward the light in yourself rather than into darkness.

Integrate your notes into your drafts and then read them aloud again. When you're satisfied that they say what you want to say and sound the way you want them to sound, think about asking someone to proofread for you.

Try asking your listeners or your proofreader to suggest titles for your drafts. The titles they propose are likely to reflect what they see as the theme of your writing, interpretations that can be surprising and that sometimes increase your self-understanding. Remember though that you as the author have the right to override suggestions of every sort.

As you write your final drafts, don't hesitate to make major changes. Final versions are sometimes quite different from first drafts and are much better.

Save your writing ideas, the notes you made about activities you enjoy, and your list of hardships in your greenhouse file. Now or at a later date, write additional chapters about your struggles and satisfactions.

Here's a bonus to play with: You've been writing to warm-up prompts. For a change, and to see what will happen, take time today to write to this "cooldown" prompt:

• I like/don't like to think about . . .

This prompt can lead you in interesting directions. Play with its various possibilities to see where it takes you.

> Success is never final; failure is never fatal; it is courage that counts.
> WINSTON CHURCHILL
> ENGLISH POLITICIAN AND HISTORIAN

You're rapidly accumulating chapters about critical aspects of your life. You've worked through a third of the chapters in this book, so at this time enjoy rereading all the narratives you've written so far. You may begin to notice themes, and you may also be surprised by insights.

If you are writing in a fellowship of writers, this would be a good time to schedule a special session at which everyone reads one chapter to the group at large. Bring any chapter you feel inclined to share, but if you prefer to just listen, feel free to say "I pass" when your turn comes round.

Before the reading begins, remind all participants to suspend judgment about the life or thoughts of the writer, listen to expand their own understanding, and guard the writer's confidentiality.

Share refreshments and celebrate your achievement.

CHAPTER ELEVEN

Focusing on Your Subject

Writing teaches us our mysteries.

MARIE DE L'INCARNATION

FOUNDER OF THE URSULINE RELIGIOUS ORDER IN CANADA

Often we give only scanty labels to the snapshots we stick in albums. Years later, descendants will look at the photographs and wonder about the lives of the people pictured. If only someone who knew the subjects had written about them! What were the dreams and fears behind the smiling faces? What mischief did each person concoct? What is the story about the horse on the other side of a fence? Why is the shack at the water's edge important? A story lies behind every photograph.

The second and possibly more lengthy draft you'll write during this chapter will be about a snapshot. But first, warm up to writing.

Find your fluency by writing quickly and impulsively from one of the following prompts. Be indifferent to mechanical correctness, and allow your writing to include whatever memories come. Here is a choice of prompts:

- A happy period in my life was when . . .
- I felt self-confident when . . .
- A time in my life I like to remember is . . .

When you finish writing, sit back and look over the story you related. Do you now see that happy period as part of a greater context? How has that period affected your life? Consider adding information to this rough draft to provide an overview.

The account you just wrote may be so pleasant to hear that you'll want to reminisce by reading it to a friend.

Pour lemonade and sit on a porch together as you hear each other's drafts. Or, if the weather is wintery, sip hot cider indoors as you savor the happy memories.

Now you're ready to move on to your second draft. This time you'll write about a snapshot picturing something, someone, or some place that has been significant in your life. You may have been any age when the picture was taken. The more important the subject is to you, the stronger your writing will be.

It might show:
- people you've known
- you at a certain time
- a meaningful place
- an experience
- a thing
- some other subject that is important to you

Telling someone about the snapshot is an excellent and natural way to prepare to write. In the telling, you'll automatically find the right words and begin to arrange your thoughts, so before you begin to write, show your snapshot to a friend or writing partner. Talk first about the photo, and then discuss the following topics:
- Everything shown in the picture
- Things *not* shown in the picture
  the time and place
  the relationships between the subject and other people
  the story behind the picture
  related stories this picture suggests
- Your own feelings about the subject in the picture
  the way you felt when the picture was taken
  reasons why you saved this photograph
  reasons why you selected it today

When you write your rough draft, it's possible that your writing will spread far beyond the scene of your photo to a greater story. Let your writing take you where it will.

Glance through your written draft to see if you indicated your feelings toward the subject. Your feelings may be indirectly indicated or stated directly.

Consider how your narrative fits into the whole of your life.

Read this draft aloud to yourself, to a writing partner, or to a small group of writing companions.

If family members read what you wrote, sooner or later someone is sure to say, "You've got it wrong. It wasn't like that at all. I'll tell you how it really was." Then that person will proceed to tell how she remembers it.

Who's to say which of you is correct? Maybe neither of you. Maybe both of you. Actually, the facts don't matter. What matters is the way *you* remember it. After all, these are your memoirs. If your memory does differ from some objective facts, that in itself is interesting. Memoirs are by their nature subjective, not objective. As some insightful person said, "Don't let the facts get in the way of the truth."

William Zinsser, an author and authority on writing, wrote: "After *Five Boyhoods* came out, my mother set me straight. 'Grandma wasn't really like that,' she said, defending the mother-in-law who had made her own life far from easy. 'She was unhappy and really quite shy, and she very much wanted to be liked.' Maybe so; the truth is somewhere between my mother's version and mine. But she was like that to me— and that's the only truth that the writer of a memoir can work with."

If you invite a family member to listen and respond to your rough draft, be prepared to stand by your story as you remember it. Revise and complete your writing before allowing it to be seen by any relatives or other people who may react with antagonism; their objections could dishearten and dissuade you. Jane Tompkins, author of *A Life in School: What the Teacher Learned,* mailed the manuscript of her memoirs to her editor before sending a copy to her mother. This sequence proved prudent because when Jane's mother received her copy, she responded with an attack that lasted over two hours. Eventually most relatives do become reconciled and gain understanding of the writer.

Suppose you don't agree with the suggestions made by listeners or proofreaders. Simply thank them for their advice, and then proceed to write the final version in your own way. Trust your own knowledge and judgment.

Because you prepared to write by first telling about your snapshot, you may not feel much need to revise your rough draft; however, if you wish, you can add information, change how you said something, cross out any part you want to omit, and rearrange paragraphs or sentences.

Consider your rough draft in light of the following questions. Do take written notes in response to them, as the act of writing will further your thinking.

- What does your selection of photographs show about what you value?
- Does this chapter tell about a time of harmony or wholeness? Tell about it.
- With whom did you empathize? Why?

If you would like to have your rough draft proofread before you write the final version, ask someone to check punctuation, paragraphing, spelling, and word choice.

Include your photograph in this chapter. Decide whether to lay out your text leaving room for the photograph at the top, under the title, or between paragraphs within the chapter. Write a caption under the picture, even though you gave identifying information in the body of your text. Photography shops sell acid-free, non-PVC photo-mounting products: double-stick tape strips, photo tabs, and adhesive protective photo holders. These products are suitable to use with acid-free paper.

～

We think of memoirs as being about the writer's own life, but occasionally memoirs are dictated by the subject to a writer who composes and edits the dictation. *The Autobiography of Malcolm X* was dictated by Malcolm X but written by Alex Haley. A similar extension of authorship occurs when a writer who is related to the subject enters imaginatively into the identity of that person to recount his or her story, using the pronoun *I*. Thea Halo wrote as if she were her own mother in *Not Even My Name* to tell the stories of escape from Turkey she had heard her mother tell.

Lisa Arkin has undertaken to write her grandmother's memoirs, something she can do thanks to the extraordinary spiritual intimacy the two of them shared and because of Lisa's detailed knowledge of her grandmother's life. When Lisa uses the pronoun *I*, she is in the role of her grandmother. Lisa is a dancer and dance educator who specializes in the history of nineteenth- and early-twentieth-century dance.

THE FRANCESCA

Yaneh and I had waited in Warsaw many, many months for the permission to leave Poland. I don't remember the details of the bureaucratic process. I only remember the endless waiting. Who in the government decides which desperate Jew gets a visa? How many bribes does it take to get the steamer ticket to leave Europe? How do the lucky ones get from Warsaw to a seaport? These questions tumbled over and over in my mind until I could think of nothing else. We pushed on every door, begged every official, sat in every waiting room until the benches and the lines and the faces behind the counters blurred together.

Somehow, we made it happen. We left our homeland behind us.

The Francesca—*this was the name of the steamer on the tickets I clutched inside the pocket of my coat during the long train ride to Italy. An Italian boat, the* Francesca *sounded to us like a bronze-skinned, dark-eyed Mediterranean maiden, a young strong woman who would take us into her arms and carry us to a better life.*

When we climbed aboard the Francesca *as she was docked in the harbor, the smell of cow manure, a pungent residue of her most recent passengers, assaulted us. By the time all of the new passengers had been taken aboard, we realized that we would fare much the same as our predecessors. It was so crowded, and we all jammed together on the deck of this freighter to avoid going below to the cattle hold. There you would be overcome by thick air redolent with hay and dung. Later, as the days passed on the* Francesca, *we would almost get used to it. The Italian crew had no patience for bewildered passengers who tugged at their sleeves with incomprehensible questions spoken in strange European languages.*

Yaneh took ill almost immediately and spent the entire voyage lying unresponsive in a dark corner of the hold. He visibly weakened day by day. . . .

Yaneh clung to life during the three weeks we sailed across the ocean in the Francesca. *When the passengers began calling out*

"America! America!" he begged me to help him crawl to the deck to see this long-awaited sight. The joy and exhilaration we felt upon seeing the Statue of Liberty erased all our previous sorrows and fears. The Francesca *docked just beyond her, near Ellis Island. Dozens of sallow yet hopeful faces peered over the railing, and somehow we all found the strength to clutch our suitcases and bundles. Our voices were light with laughter as people talked about the relatives that would be waiting to welcome them to America. The end of the long journey and the beginning of a new life was within our grasp.*

But although the lady of liberty had beckoned, America's doors were closed to us. The Francesca's *cargo of Eastern Europeans, many of us Jewish, was not allowed under America's new immigration quotas. Our type of people was being counted, checked, and bound to strict limitations. They've already reached their quota of Jews this year, we were told.*

When the boat began to pull away from the dock a wailing rose amongst us. Arms stretched over the railings and hands reached out to the majestic lady who had promised "Give me your tired, your poor, your hungry. . . ." Some men helped me bring Yaneh below. His eyes were glassy. None of us spoke. As the New York skyline grew smaller and smaller, the despair that settled over us crushed our spirits. The Francesca *met the open sea again.*

～

If you wrote about a person with whom you are still in contact, consider sending a copy of this chapter to your subject. He or she will be surprised and, if your memories are positive, pleased.

If you wrote about a place or thing, think about whether the people who were there with you or who knew you at the time when the snapshot was taken would enjoy reading your account. It's likely that the people who were personally involved will take an interest in it.

Be warned that the recipient of your chapter will find discrepancies between your memories and hers, and be assured that your memories are as valid as those of anyone else. Know that someone is likely to challenge even a trivial detail. Be prepared to smile to yourself, and keep writing.

CHAPTER TWELVE

Transitions

The art of progress is to preserve order amid change and to preserve change amid order.

ALFRED NORTH WHITEHEAD

ENGLISH MATHEMATICIAN AND PHILOSOPHER

Before you gather ideas for your next chapter, warm up with some rapid writing. The warm-up writing primes your mind in the same way an athlete's warm-up prepares her body for an event. Write as much as you can in about twenty minutes. Use one of the following prompts, or make up your own:

- A time when I felt optimistic and hopeful was when . . .
- A time when doors were opening for me . . .
- I looked forward to . . .

If you would enjoy sharing this draft with friends, read it to your supper companions this evening or read it over the telephone to a friend or relative. Explain that you've undertaken a major writing project and that this reminiscence is part of it.

> If you're writing with colleagues, do not break into small groups this time, but sit back and savor everyone's stories. Of course, you'll remember to withhold judgments, listen to broaden your understanding, and keep the readers' revelations within the group.
>
> Point out the best aspect of each person's writing, and ask about something not completely evident.

Sometimes the warm-up writing develops into a piece more major than the second composition. Always allow your writing to be as lengthy or short as feels appropriate.

If you're writing independently, go ahead at this time to expand your rough draft, revise it, proofread it, give it a title, and write your final version. If you're writing with a partner or circle of writers, set this draft aside to complete when you're alone.

～

This excerpt is from the memoirs of Dr. Tim Brinton. Though he ends this section at the time when he became a janitor, he eventually went to medical school and became an anesthesiologist. These days he enjoys fast downhill skiing.

My feelings on leaving home were not regret nor longing, but rather a quiet determination to prove that I could be independent, that I could support myself, and that I could "get an education." I had been away from home before for periods of up to a month, always with friends. Leaving home was an easy adjustment. I was busy with my new life as a college student. I hardly looked back toward home in Baker forty miles away. After about six weeks I returned home for a weekend visit and to pick up additional possessions. Dad said, "You've changed."

He acknowledged the independence that I was proving to myself. With an exchange of glances and a pause and without more words, Dad and I both understood what was not spoken. My home ties were separated. I had passed into an adult stage of my life. Dad was uncomfortable speaking about feelings and personal matters, but he was sensitive to people.

Mother asked about my laundry, my winter jacket, did I have enough bedding. She had ready cookies and home-canned fruit for my return to La Grande.

My brother Jim had just preceded me as a student at Eastern Oregon College. I joined with some of his student friends who were "baching it" in an apartment. We learned the realities of cooking and washing dishes and cleaning. Our odds and ends of dishes and utensils were barely enough to fry eggs and heat canned beans or stew. Our convenience foods consisted of home-canned fruit or jam. One roommate from a farm home occasionally received meat or chicken which we shared. Our menu was limited by our inexperience in planning and cooking.

After a few weeks I started a part-time job as a janitor in the Green Parrot Grill. . . .

There is nothing permanent except change.
HERACLITUS
EARLY GREEK PHILOSOPHER

Sometimes we initiate changes in our lives, but frequently they are imposed on us by external circumstances. Transitions can be beneficial or harmful. They can be seen as curses or blessings, and sometimes in retrospect, we alter our evaluation of them.

To prepare to write about a transition in your life, first list changes you've experienced. Write them down as they occur to you, and move freely back and forth between the following categories: geographic changes, economic changes, changes in family structure, career changes, changes in relationships and changes in friends, changes in health or physical condition, changes in interests, changing affiliations or memberships, changing beliefs or values. Leave six, eight, or more lines under each heading.

From the changes you listed, circle the two that seem most dramatic or that have had the greatest impact on you—or about which you feel inclined to write. Then place your list of changes in your greenhouse file.

Find a partner. If you're writing independently, invite a friend to join you for coffee and to hear about two of the changes you've experienced. If you're more comfortable confiding in the cat, then talk to your cat about transitions. Explaining the changes aloud before you write will boost your written fluency.

Choose one of the two stories you just related. When you told them, you probably found that one seemed more significant than the other or would develop as a chapter better than the other. Or, you might have found that you felt more inclined to write about one subject than the other.

Scrawl a quick, sloppy draft and then follow the process you now know well for listening to it and receiving responses.

~

This memory of a child's move to college is from a mother's perspective. The writer, Wanda Henson, is a nurse, teacher, and volunteer supporter of her local art museum and county government. She considers herself fortunate to have the freedom to pursue her many interests.

> *We took our oldest son, Larry, up to McMinnville to help him get settled in his dorm at Linfield College. It brought back memories of when I first arrived at my own dorm and how excited I was. Leaving Larry up there was not so emotionally draining as it might have been, because my memories helped me to be excited for him starting this new adventure.*
>
> *Monday I came home from school and started dinner. As usual, my final act of dinner preparation was setting the table. To my surprise, I couldn't set the table in the dining room that evening, because Larry wasn't in there playing the piano. The first thing he always did when he arrived home from school was go to the piano. I could tell how he was feeling, what kind of day he'd had by the songs he played, or the way he played them. To my surprise, I started crying and couldn't set the table. We ate in the kitchen for almost two weeks before I could bring myself to go in the dining room and set just four places at the table.*
>
> *Until that Monday evening, the awareness that our family had changed forever hadn't hit me. We were still a family, but it would now be different.*

~

Reflect on the account you wrote. To make your reflection as insightful as possible, write notes in response to the following questions:
- How were you changed by the transition?
- What resources helped you make the change?
- Where did you find your courage? Resilience? Energy? Patience?
- How was the change beneficial? Detrimental?
- Was destiny involved? Do you believe in destiny?

When you revise your rough draft, use arrows to indicate any re-arrangement of paragraphs you'd like to make. If you plan to insert additional paragraphs, place numbered asterisks where you will insert correspondingly numbered paragraphs. Change words or phrases and strike out sentences or paragraphs you don't like.

After you've proofread your revised draft and given it a title, find documents and photographs from the time you described. Clippings, saved letters, and scrapbook souvenirs all add interest and life to written accounts. Records of any sort give a sense of authenticity and add the flavor of the time. Photography shops and even copy shops can often improve the clarity of old photographs, so consider using these photographs even if they're not now in good condition.

Thirty-Three

Knowing others is wisdom;
Knowing the self is enlightenment.
Mastering others requires force;
Mastering the self needs strength.

He who knows he has enough is rich.
Perseverance is a sign of will power.
He who stays where he is endures.
To die but not to perish is to be eternally present.

LAO TSU, CHINESE PHILOSOPHER

TAO TE CHING, SIXTH CENTURY B.C.

CHAPTER THIRTEEN

Joinings and Separations

Every parent should be charged with recounting and sharing personal memories about their children's first hours. Not just the commonplace details we're asked to fill in on the lined-off spaces of commercially produced baby books, but sentiments and particulars of the kind [this book, *Families Writing*] captures.

PETER R. STILLMAN

AMERICAN WRITER, EDITOR, TEACHER

In this session you'll write about the arrival of a new person in your life or the loss of someone. You might write about a birth, a death, a first encounter, or a parting. Often we lose people for reasons other than death; nevertheless those individuals leave our lives just as certainly as if they had died.

Focus on the actual moments of first coming together or on the event of separating. You might have been any age when the experience occurred. Many of us retain pictures in our minds: a newcomer appearing at the door; the back of a man as he walks away; a child peering from behind a window, waving; the irregular breaths, and the last breath, of a dying person.

Gain writing momentum with a quick warm-up. Choose one of the following two prompts or an alternative:

• The first time I saw . . .
• The last time I saw . . .

As alternatives to writing about the first time or last time you saw a certain person, you could write about a place or an object. Still another kind of alternative is to use a sense other than vision. You might write, "The last time I heard . . ." or "The first time I felt. . . ." As soon as you decide on your prompt, write impulsively and rapidly.

Dana Furgerson is a teacher, writer, and wood-carver. Her son, now in his thirties, grew up to become a potter.

> *The birth of my son triggered emotions of such profound intensity that I remember them with exquisite clarity. Dear God, the first instant I saw my baby boy I knew what mother love was. Its fierce intensity charged through me. I felt as if the nurse who placed my baby in my arms had also handed me a sword to wield against the world.*
>
> *I knew the importance of the life in my arms far exceeded mine. I would die for my baby. I would kill, if need be. I knew I could never alter this love or diminish it. I cried for joy, but a terror of the magnitude of my feelings invaded me. I was a strong woman, a struggling survivor of a pervasive, damaging mother. I knew what decisions I made at this moment would shape both my son's and my life. I pledged to guide my son toward independence from me. I pledged to honor his being as separate from mine. But most of all, I promised my son that I wouldn't repeat what had been done to me.*
>
> *The fear of becoming my mother smothered me, and an iciness enveloped my chest. I held my boy to me and chanted, "I love you, son. I love you." I would not be like my mother. I knew this now. I swung my imaginary sword and vanquished all that threatened my boy and me. I chuckled with joy. My boy, my boy.*

Read your rough draft aloud to a friend who is present with you or to a friend who is with you in your memory.

> **If you are with a community of writers, read to those friends. After you acknowledge each co-writer's primary talent, ask a question formulated to help the writer add supportive information.**

You're ready to gather subjects for your next chapter.

Throughout our lives we acquire new associates, friends, antagonists, and family members, and we lose people, too. Separations from them may fill us with either grief or relief. Prepare to write about people who entered into or departed from your life by listing:

- Births with which you've been closely associated.
- Close friends or relatives who have died. Give their names if you were with them or near them at the time of their deaths.
- Animals whose deaths or disappearances affected you. The slaughter of a farm animal can be a painful memory.
- If you remember the occasions when you first encountered people who became significant in your life, list those people.
- If you remember the times of separation from people who were important to you, list those people. Perhaps you lost a friend when your family moved, when a friendship ruptured, or when the personality of one of you changed. Mental illness or impairment and addictions can sever close companions, and the separation of divorce often leaves vivid final memories. Take time to list people you lost from various causes.

Many of the incidents behind the names you listed are subjects for important chapters. Choose any one of them to write about now. If you feel inclined to write about an experience that looks trivial in comparison with others, go ahead and do so. Your responses to the death of a pet or some other lesser-seeming experience may reveal a significant dimension in yourself.

When you've chosen a subject for today's chapter, file your list of topics in your greenhouse folder for future writing.

～

From her home in Eugene, Oregon, Sharon Franklin prepares textbooks for publication. She wrote these thoughts about her dog, Evie, and about herself:

> *I miss Evie terribly. I miss the way she leaned into my body and let me stroke her bony little back. I miss the way she would throw her head back and look at me. I miss the way she put her paw on my foot as if to say "I belong to you!" or snap her lips and teeth together in anticipation of a treat.*
>
> *Evie showed me the best part of myself. She reminded me that I*

am not too busy to help someone I love. She showed me that sacrifice means nothing. It's just what you do. Evie also was, I think, symbolic of some abandoned part of myself. I learned to love that part.

Though Sharon was writing about her dog, she has shown us even more about herself.

⌣

Prepare to write by talking with a friend or relative about the incident you've chosen. If you kept a diary at the time of the incident, look at it to see what you wrote.

This narrative could begin or end with a detailed scene. To create that scene, see the techniques suggested in chapter four. Since your chapter will probably involve telling why your subject was important to you, you are likely to relate a story that precedes and follows the detailed scene you show.

> **Find a partner and tell each other about the subjects you are considering.**

After you've explored your subject conversationally, write a quick first draft.

⌣

The following excerpt is taken from the memoirs of Sara Schwake, whose writing you glimpsed in the chapter about childhood. It is from a chapter about her mother's last days.

. . . the last E.R. sojourn, where there was "little to be done but keep her comfortable," made me know it was completely right to place her gently in our car for her last ride. I got in the backseat and put my arms around her shoulders as Alan drove. She was conscious but unable to verbalize. Still, I wanted to show her something of the beauty in the scruffy, mostly barren eastern Oregon landscape. I told her to look at the rims of mountain ranges surrounding us with pale

pink light in the late afternoon dusk. They were miles away, but she slowly turned to look. It's OK, Mom . . . we're going for a drive . . . together we've enjoyed this so many times before.

～

Hear the effect of your rough draft by reading it to a kind, appreciative listener or to your circle of writers. Ask listeners to respond according to the now familiar guidelines.

～

In the following excerpt, Leila McMillan Shaw describes the death of her mother, a forerunner of the first women to take leading rolls in the Presbyterian Church. Copies of Leila's book have been placed in national and local Presbyterian libraries.

Leila included many photographs from her family's album. She located a copy shop where a clerk helped her make good duplications by adjusting the exposure and contrast.

In early March Mother was very ill with congestion of the lungs. My sister, Juanita, let me know that I should come as soon as possible. I completed school reports due and flew to Arkansas.

Mother got out of bed to greet me when I came into her room. Her illness had caused her to lose the extra weight she had gained in her latter years. Spontaneously I exclaimed,

"Mother, you're so beautiful!"

She with matching spontaneity replied, "Oh, pooh," dismissing the compliment.

Juanita helped Mother put on her robe and slippers, and we sat on the porch to visit and enjoy the warm spring day.

The next morning I sat by Mother's bed as she alternately dozed and waked. She asked whether the hyacinths were in bloom. I went to the garden and found a pink one in full flower. When I brought the hyacinth to Mother, she said, "And they will bloom again next year."

Those were her last words to me.

Though you "hear" Leila's mother speak only one phrase and the exclamation "Oh, pooh," notice how much dimension her voice adds to our sense of her.

—

Revise your rough draft as much or as little as is appropriate for your purposes. People writing solely for themselves often find personal satisfaction in the improvements that result from revision.

The following suggestions may help you:

• Aural perceptions. If in reading your draft aloud you heard anything you wanted to change, take care of that first.

• Listeners' responses. If the questions from your listeners have made you aware of ways you can strengthen the writing, take care of that too.

• Showing through actions. Actions, also, can reflect feelings—a gentle gesture or a harsh act indicates emotion. During a previous session you described a snapshot. This time visualize your experience as if it were a movie. Add movement.

• Dialogue. The use of dialogue is a very good way to show feelings. Try to find places where you can insert approximations of the words spoken. Interweave descriptions of the action with dialogue.

• Sensory description. Most of us tell how things looked, but we often forget to use our other senses. Yet smells and textures give readers a sense of presence. See if there are places in your draft where you can include smells, sounds, the sense of touch, and possibly even tastes.

• Metaphysical or philosophical meaning. You may or may not want to interpret your narrative overtly. Your description is already likely to show the energies within the experience. It might even suggest a sense of transcendence.

This narrative may be embellished by the addition of diary or journal accounts, photographs, newspaper announcements, certificates, farewell letters, or trinkets associated with the entry or exit of your subject.

—

The following lament was written by a seven- or eight-year-old child who experienced separation when a favorite tree was felled. It's from the diary of Opal Whiteley, a precocious girl who grew up in the early 1900s in logging settlements near Cottage Grove, Oregon. Opal used colored crayons to print her diary on odd sheets of paper given to her by a neighbor. Editors corrected spelling and added punctuation at a later date.

Some Day I will write about
the great tree that I love.
Today I did watch
and I did hear its moans
as the saw went through it.
There was a queer feel in my throat
and I couldn't stand up.
All the woods seemed still
except the pain-sound of the saw.
It seemed like a little voice
was calling from the cliffs.
And then it was many voices.
They were all little voices calling
as one silver voice came together.
The saw—it didn't stop—
it went on sawing.
Then I did have thinks
the silver voice was calling
to the soul of the big tree.
The saw did stop.
There was a stillness.
There was a queer sad sound.
The big tree did quiver
It did sway.
It crashed to earth.
Oh, Michael Raphael!

OPAL: THE JOURNAL OF AN UNDERSTANDING HEART

ADAPTED BY JANE BOULTON

CHAPTER FOURTEEN
Chance and Choice

The future is a place that is created—created first in the mind and will, created next in activity. The paths are not to be found but made, and the activity making them changes both the maker and the destination.

DR. JOHN H. SCHAAR

PROFESSOR AND AUTHOR, UNIVERSITY OF CALIFORNIA

SANTA CRUZ

We work hard to achieve our goals and we construct our lives as best we can, but we also succumb to events beyond our control. Throughout our lives we interact with chance. Like partners dancing, we lead part of the time, but our partner, Chance, swings and turns us and changes our steps. Wisdom lies in knowing how much to lead, how much to follow—and how to find beatitude wherever the dance takes us.

⁓

You're about to write about the interplay of choice and chance and acceptance of outcomes, but first, warm up to writing.

Paying no attention to mechanical correctness, write impulsively and freely from the following prompt:

- I had to make a difficult decision when . . .

We've all had to make difficult decisions, but if your decision was too agonizing to write about today, file this prompt to use when you are ready. It's a powerful prompt that will lead deep into the story of your soul. If you are not ready to travel inward this far, write instead to the following prompt:

- A choice I'm glad/sorry I made . . .

Alone, with a partner, or in a small group, read aloud about the difficult decision you made. Today, in similar circumstances, you might make a different decision. Remind your listener or listeners to be sensitive to your frailties and to remember that you told about an especially trying time in your life.

As we listen to each other's stories, it is best to assume that we have all made mistakes and to remember that our decisions were based on past circumstances and understandings. Suggest that your listeners respond by commenting on the strengths in your writing and asking a question designed to evoke more information.

Prepare for further writing. On a fresh sheet of paper, write two lists in columns, one down the left side of the paper, the other down the right side. Entitle one list "Fortunate Experiences" and the other "Unfortunate Experiences." Then name your experiences in the two columns in whatever order they occur to you.

After you have made your lists, you may notice something curious. Not uncommonly, the same experience appears on both lists. If an event that at first appeared to be disastrous brought certain benefits in the long run, then it is both disastrous and beneficial. An opportunity lost may have motivated someone to find a satisfying alternative. Adversity or suffering may have taught certain important skills. Some writers have felt new appreciation for their lives when they survived serious illness or disability. A fortunate outcome does not invalidate the unfortunate aspect.

In the same way, fortunate experiences sometimes sour. A promotion, a marriage, a discovery, even a windfall can all have unexpected dark sides. You will have to decide whether to place such events on one or both lists.

> Life is a series of collisions with the future; it is not a sum of what we have been but what we yearn to be.
>
> JOSÉ ORTEGA Y GASSET
>
> SPANISH PHILOSOPHER AND ESSAYIST

Consider telling a friend about one of your more influential experiences. Perhaps you can bring it up casually while you eat a meal together or talk on the telephone. Initiate the conversation by mentioning that you've been remembering a time when. . . .

Fortunate Experiences	Unfortunate Experiences
piano lessons	house fire
Jessica's friendship	losing piano
Mom's new job	Mom not at home
big recital	Dad's girlfriend
date to prom	Shawn's ulcer
scholarship	debts
meeting Ashley	allergies
pregnancy	pregnancy
my sales job	dropping out of school
promotion	Mom + Dad's divorce
taking in Shawn	taking in Shawn
Ashley's patience	Shawn's arrest
move to Nebraska	low-wage job
promotion	car broke down
Shawn's job	debts
big garden	Ashley's depression
new job	no health insurance
bought piano	no vacation time
Ashley's improvement	Dad's stroke
bought insurance.	
trip to New Mexico	
joined writers' group	

If you are writing with fellow writers, find a partner. Tell your partner about any one of the fortunate experiences and any one of the unfortunate experiences.

Listen while your partner does the same thing.

Write your rough draft.

The ways in which we cope with adversity are frequently more revealing than the ways in which we respond to happy circumstances, so consider writing about a time that tested you. Furthermore, although we don't often enjoy writing about our failures, doing so shows much about ourselves and, rather than alienating readers, tends to draw them closer to us. Revelation of our weaknesses and flaws usually humanizes us to our readers.

To make your writing vivid, recall the most emotional moments of the experience. Visualize yourself in a particular place at a certain time; describe what you saw, heard, smelled, felt, thought, and did. Be as specific as possible. If you can remember what someone is likely to have said or what you said, add quotations.

Read your rough draft aloud, listening to it as if it were written by someone else whom you love.

~

Doug Finn, author of the following account, describes himself as "a musician, a writer, a husband, and a father who has lived for fifty-six years and is still trying to figure out what it's all about."

> *The motor puttered and the wind washed over my face, whipping my clothes against my body. It was a little 180cc Yamaha that I had bought about six months ago—about five months before Barb told me I should leave, that she didn't want to live with me anymore. I cried then. It was the only time she or our daughter, Heather, had ever seen me cry. Heather was only four. I doubt that she remembers that now.*
>
> *I loved the wind against me. I loved the feeling of being enclosed by nothing, the sky for a ceiling, the ground for a floor. I was on a little dirt road that ran up into the mountains west of Tucson. I had*

already left the desert behind and now the trees were oaks and pines. The dust rolled up behind me and filtered into my nose with a dry, musty smell. It was hot. I wore jeans and a T-shirt and a small, white helmet.

I could take the road pretty fast, thirty-five or forty, except where the curves were sharp. The road wound around, climbing steadily, and it was full of rocks. The vibration numbed my hands and made my forearms tingle.

Divorce was imminent and devastating. We had been married five years. We had shared life, made a baby, taken care of each other, each in our own way. I didn't know what she wanted, but she had become the center of my love, and thinking about life without her was looking over a cliff into black, cold, empty space.

The sun was shining, the green oak leaves shuddered in a slight breeze. On my left the mountain rose almost straight up, and on my right it dropped almost straight down, and there was no reason to live. I was alone. I hadn't seen another human for over two hours, since I left the outskirts of Tucson. I would be alone now, and I couldn't live that way. There was nothing to live for. And all of this, the trees, the sun, the sky, the wind, wasn't enough. I needed to share it.

I knew how easy it would be. Just don't lean, don't turn. Get the speed up to forty or fifty, and at the next left turn, go straight.

I had no brilliant illumination. God didn't speak to me. I didn't come to realize that my life was worth living after all. I just didn't do it. I carried my despair back down the mountain, back to the city, back to my job and all the mundaneness of my life, and in some ways that despair is still with me today.

But I made a decision. I exercised my free will. I went on. And the part of the stream of life that my life has touched since that time has been different because of me.

⌣

The draft you've just written may lend itself to deeper examination than have previous drafts. If you'd like to ponder it, respond when you can to the following suggestions. Some may not work with your draft but others will. Write about:

- What you learned from the experience
- Qualities found, such as resolution, compassion, sacrifice, and service
- What, in retrospect, you observe about yourself
- Instances of
  creativity
  intuition
  inspiration
  the animating force, the source of your strength
  any instance of mercy
  grace
  compassion
- Ways the experience affected your doubts and beliefs
- What significance this experience has had in your life
- Whether at any time during the experience you had a sense of transformation

If you want to cut pages of your rough draft apart to make room to insert additional paragraphs, do so.

Get rid of the tendency
to judge yourself
above, below, or
equal to others.
    ABHIRUPA-NANDA
    BUDDHIST NUN, SIXTH CENTURY B.C.

Now is the time to think of a title for your narrative. The reason why titles may best be written last is because we don't know exactly what we'll say or what its impact will be until after we've completed the writing.

Enhance your final version with documents. Consider adding letters, photographs, entries from your journal, or other documents. If you have kept a journal, lift portions from it to insert directly into this selection. Journal entries written at the time of a past experience will inject a strong sense of immediacy and will also show the person you were at that time.

⌣

The following excerpt is from the recently completed memoirs of Joanne Randolph. She had ten copies made for members of her family, but now additional relatives and friends want copies of her book, so she's returning to the copy shop to make more.

For days after the surgery, reports would dribble in, saying this or that test was negative, no problem. And then we'd wait for the next results of other tests. My tension would build up and then explode in tears, and my dear husband would simply hold me until I was all cried out. Then I'd feel strangely peaceful and able to go on.

My massage therapist was wonderful, but not able to break through my fear and tension; I couldn't sleep without drugs, couldn't breathe naturally. I was full of tension, so she sent me to an acupuncturist she knew.

In one session he improved my breathing and in the second, my sleeping. But it was his great Jewish wisdom that healed me as much as his acupuncture. He told me I was strong and I denied it, and he said, "You're here, you're strong." He said I had just lost my confidence in myself and needed to let go and just jump. "There's good stuff on the other side of this, but you have to punch your way through." He said more, but this is what impressed my memory so deeply.

My fight back to normalcy—and beyond—started that day. Shortly after, I joined a twelve-step program, "Adult Children of Alcoholics," and for five years gently prodded myself to look back on painful times and heal them. It's a long process, but it helped me let go of some faulty conclusions I had made about myself. From ACOA I went on to Co-Dependents Anonymous and started to learn why I was a "people pleaser" even when I was hurting myself in the process.

. . . My husband says I'm easier to live with now, though my changes have caused some changes in him. He says he couldn't figure where I was coming from before, and now he can, at least sometimes.

Everything has a price, I guess. My life is so positive and enjoyable now, any price isn't too high.

About five years after my surgery, a question popped into my head: If I could have my breast back by giving up the wisdom and peace I had acquired, would I want to go back? I didn't know the answer. When another year had passed, I knew: I would never want to go back.

～

If you have not yet completed the warm-up writing, look back at that rough draft. Reflect on the difficult decision you had to make:

• Can you discern how the experience affected your life? If so, add thoughts about this.

• Was there any time in the experience when you had a sense of transcendence or of being in touch with something larger than yourself?

• In what ways did external events and your self-determination interact?

Follow the same process of revising, proofreading, and writing a final version that you used when you wrote about the fortunate or unfortunate experience.

Toward the end of his life, my father, twice a widower, married again. Shortly after the wedding, my new stepmother, whom he had known for only a few months, began to show signs of dementia. My father had macular degeneration, and caring for a spouse with dementia was extremely difficult. I was concerned about him, and I gently asked if he felt he had to take care of someone he had not known long. His answer was reproachful but instructive: "How many ways can a blind eighty-seven-year-old be useful in this world? Of course I will take care of her!"

JAMES E. SABIN

PROFESSOR OF PSYCHIATRY, HARVARD MEDICAL SCHOOL

CHAPTER FIFTEEN

Aspirations

When I am . . . completely myself, entirely alone . . . or during the night when I cannot sleep, it is on such occasion that my ideas flow best and most abundantly. Whence and how these come I know not nor can I force them.

WOLFGANG AMADEUS MOZART
AUSTRIAN MUSICIAN AND COMPOSER

We have all set goals and dreamed dreams, and we've succeeded in realizing some of them. From the time we were young children, we've had notions about what we wanted to be when we grew up and about the kind of people we wanted to become. Our ideas have shifted many times as we realized what was possible and as our interests and inclinations changed; furthermore, as long as we are healthy and vital, we continue to aspire toward new purposes.

Though we find satisfaction in our accomplishments, many of our good intentions, dreams, and strivings never become manifest. They are likely not even to be apparent, and yet they are the greater part of our efforts. Like the underwater bulk of an iceberg, most of our aspirations are out of sight. Only our closest confidants and we ourselves know what we would like to have achieved.

As you write this chapter, you'll make visible an important part of yourself as you confide your intentions and dreams.

Today you'll first capture ideas. On a full sheet of paper, draw the outline of a large cloud. Inside the cloud name the goals you've had from childhood up to the present time. Include present aspirations. You may randomly place the words you write in the cloud. Name your dreams in the following categories: vocational, professional, athletic, artistic, social and political, ecological, related to family and friends, domestic, related to self-improvement.

Add your particular dreams that go beyond these categories.

If you had a difficult childhood, you may not have had an opportunity to dream and formulate aspirations when you were young. Some children are so overwhelmed with simply surviving that their intentions must focus on the immediate situation. If your childhood was like that, then your cloud may not be as full as the cloud of someone who had a comfortable, well-nurtured childhood. You are to be commended for any aspirations you managed to generate.

Write about your aspirations, starting with one of the following prompts or by beginning in your own way:

- One of my aspirations has been to . . .
- I wanted to be/become/be like . . .
- A goal I've had . . .

Read your rough draft aloud to yourself, to a friend, or to a small group of writers.

~

Marlene Elam Neal never did become a champion swimmer, but she is now a member of a theater troupe in Oakridge, Oregon, called Zero Clearance. Here is an excerpt from her chapter "Swimming."

I was about nine years old when Red Cross swimming lessons were coming to town in that summer. There had been many articles in my Weekly Reader *at school that I was faithfully practicing so I would be prepared for the river. I dived for marbles in the bathroom sink, retrieving them with my teeth. I took my baths all in total immersion with my eyes wide open. I flutter kicked and Australian crawled with my belly touching nothing but the piano bench. I saw every Esther Williams movie available in my small town. Mother fastened my braids on top of my head; I was ready.*

Ferne M. Kellow is a teacher and avid genealogist who enriches her charts with stories about family members who might otherwise be known by no more than their names.

Though Ferne was discouraged from pursuing a teaching career, she went on to earn a Ph.D. and has taught at all levels, from kindergarten through graduate school. She says the obstacles in her own life have made her a good tutor of students who contend with difficulties.

I went to Southern Oregon State College on a full scholarship—determined to become a teacher—never dreaming that my teeth might prevent me from fulfilling that dream.

Dr. Smith was my freshman speech teacher and broke the bad news to me the day I gave my first speech. After class she spoke to me in the hall, saying, "The College will never certify you as an elementary teacher with a lisp as bad as yours." Lisp? No one had ever told me before that I had a speech impediment. To say that I was shocked is putting it mildly. The only suggestion Dr. Smith had was special speech classes.

For three years I took remedial speech training for no credit. At the end of my junior year that teacher told me, "Your lisp is impossible to correct. You're doing everything right, but the gaps between your teeth just let the air through. I'm sorry. We can't approve you for student teaching." The silent screaming in my head started again.

But I've always been stubborn and don't take being told I can't do something lightly. So, I set out to find a dentist who could put in an extra tooth and fill in the offending gap. The first dentist I found said that he would do it for around one thousand dollars, an outrageous price for a starving college student. The second dentist told me seductively, as he ran his hand up and down my leg, "I think I can help you." Naive as I was at the time, I realized that that price was even higher than the first. Finally, I discovered Dr. Thompson, a Medford orthodontist, who was horrified that the college was trying to keep me from teaching because of a problem that he thought was minor. He agreed to put braces on my teeth to correct the problem. Adults, it seemed, could have their teeth straightened. The College finally agreed that if I was willing to go through all that I could become a teacher.

No other technique for the conduct of life attaches the individual so
firmly to reality as laying emphasis on work: for his work at least gives
him a secure place in a portion of reality, in the human community.
DR. SIGMUND FREUD
AUSTRIAN PHYSICIAN AND PSYCHOLOGIST

You first captured your dreams in a cloud. Now you'll draw a trail
on which you'll trace work you've done, making a path of memories
from which to choose a subject. On a new page, draw a wide, meandering path, and along its way, name the kinds of work you have done
from childhood until now. Include:

- chores
- schoolwork
- work in the home
- training for a job
- vocational and professional work
- work for causes
- volunteer work

Then, build three pillars of words that show the people, causes, and
goals for which you have willingly donated work, time, and money. At
the top of three columns write the words "People," "Personal Goals,"
and "Causes."

Under each of these headings, list the people on whom you have
spent your effort or money, the goals you have invested in, and the
causes you have supported. You may have deferred or even sacrificed
your own needs or pleasures in order to further greater goals.

Scan the scope of your efforts and achievements. Look at the pathway
of work you have done, and then read the lists of people and goals you
furthered. As you review these lists, make notes about the specific jobs
you did and efforts you made that led to feelings of satisfaction, harmony, and proportion.

Now you are ready to write about your work and the causes you've
worked for that were satisfying or frustrating. Describe your aspirations,
attempts, rewards and outcomes, and feelings. A humble service can be

emptied trash
feed dog
lemonade stand
babysat brother
mowed grass
did homework
paper route
grocery bagger
school work
waiter at Morley's
university studies
job with Sullivan
painted house
started business
program chair
City Club
scout leader
president, Rotary
expanded business
trained Frank as V.P.
put in garden
joined League of Women Voters with Patty
volunteer reading
mentor at school
deliver meals on wheels
serve on church vestry
help Frank

as gratifying as a renowned achievement; you needn't focus only on worldly success.

Not all of our efforts are successful, but when they do make a difference in the life of an individual, and especially when our actions contribute toward improved conditions for many people, then we have the satisfaction of sharing in the work of great leaders and statesmen.

～

Debra Burgess-Mohr has written about her efforts to promote racial justice. The demonstration she describes here took place in 1967 when Jim Clark, a sheriff who had turned fire hoses and dogs on demonstrators in Selma, Alabama, came to Oregon. Debbie says, "There was a certain rage that helped me feel purposeful and determined."

High summer clouds drifted overhead on the day of our march in Eugene. I walked with Henry, Frank, and Lila as we led some fifty people: students, clergy, faculty members, a few housewives, and businessmen down Thirteenth Street on campus. We'd made our placards—CORE Congress of Racial Equality. CORE Rally Student Union 10:00 A.M. Sat.

And we sang, "We shall overcome . . . we shall overcome . . ." against the thrumming sputter of police-mounted motorcycles.

On campus we were greeted with scattered whistles and cheers. Moving on toward town, the response was mixed: puzzlement, disgust, surprise, anger, a few friendly smiles. Down on Broadway, in the heart of downtown, I saw people I knew: a couple of lawyers, an architect. The children's pediatrician watched us for a moment, waved, then went on with his business. Two women, mothers of Amy's kindergarten classmates, saw me and called out, "Hi, Debbie." I had no clue as to how they viewed this issue, but my God, I wished they cared.

We moved on to the plaza where we stood in front of a fountain where a sculpture of bronze fish leaped and flashed in the water and sun. Henry gave a rousing speech about how black Americans were

denied decent housing, jobs, and good education. He ended by outlin-
ing our plans for CORE's fund-raising events over the coming year,
all in support of the civil rights workers in the deep South. Frank
and two other U of O students, spoke about the importance of student
involvement.

Then, just as we were regrouping to start back to campus, I heard
the shouts: "Nigger lovers!" A small group, maybe a dozen men and
women holding a crudely lettered banner, White Citizens for Christ
and White Brotherhood, *stood around two pickups. An egg hit*
Henry on his arm. He ignored it. I was impressed by his cool, unbend-
ing dignity.

"Dirty commies!" one man yelled and spit at us. "Go to Russia.
We don't need your kind around here!" Frank glanced at the man
as if he were air, then he and Henry, Wally, and Roy Brown closed
ranks to take the lead and we started back up the street.

"Niggers! Go back to Africa where you belong." An egg smacked
me on the back of my head. It hurt and felt warm and runny as it
trickled down my scalp. Luv's hands tightened on mine, Henry's voice
rose and we all sang: "We shall overcome . . . we shall overcome . . .
someday . . . someday."

Alone or among other writers, read aloud your rough draft. Listeners
should know to suspend judgment, listen with an open mind, and
honor the confidence of the writer.

Ask listeners to point out the strengths in your writing and to each
ask a question.

". . . it is when you are really living in the present—working, thinking,
lost, absorbed in something you care about very much, that you are living
spiritually."

BRENDA UELAND

AMERICAN WRITER, EDITOR, TEACHER OF WRITING

To reflect on your writing, use the following suggestion: If you
prayed for help in achieving your goals, write down what you probably
said in your prayer.

Reread your rough draft, looking for instances of:
- courage
- devotion
- capability
- service
- energy
- intelligence
- intuition
- grace
- times when you allowed your self-interest to be superseded by regard for others

Revise both drafts you wrote for this chapter, have them proofread, give them titles, and write final versions.

Doing good to others is not a duty. It is a joy, for it increases your own health and happiness.

ZOROASTER

PERSIAN PROPHET

Chuck Selden has been a fish biologist, a lawyer, and a bookstore owner. He has a passion for ice hockey and still plays the game at age seventy-one. In this part of his memoirs, he remembers an effort in which he took part when he was a young soldier.

It was Christmas in Korea. The year—1951. I was a jeep driver in a medium artillery battalion. Our quarters were six miles back from the front. We had forward observers on the front line. Their job was to be on the lookout for enemy targets that could be shelled with 155mm projectiles. Those observers were not going without a full-cooked Christmas dinner if our mess sergeant could help it.

The hot food was placed in thermal murmite cans, each about the size of a lard can. We must have had five or six murmite cans. The nobility of this mission was so great that our captain, the head of intelligence, had volunteered.

We started the trek to the front in two jeeps. Things went well until we reached the last quarter mile or so. The grade alone would not stop us, but the underlying ice was to give us fits. Not even chains helped. We proceeded on foot with cans strapped on our backs, slipping, sliding, and cursing but bent upon our goal of reaching the bunker where our observers were sure to be eagerly awaiting our arrival.

Come to think of it, no one had called ahead to tell them what delight awaited if they could just hold out till we got there.

We slogged to the top. We found the bunker. We thrust back the soggy, clammy GI blanket hung for a door. There was a glow inside. We burst in with the Christmas cheer and the food.

There was total surprise. Our observers told us they had already eaten with the infantry!

Look back at the many ideas you captured for this chapter. From your cloud, your meandering path, and your lists of work for people, goals, and causes, circle subjects for future chapters. Then store these ideas in your greenhouse folder.

When people are serving, life is no longer meaningless.

JOHN W. GARDNER

AMERICAN POLITICAL ACTIVIST, FOUNDER OF COMMON CAUSE

CHAPTER SIXTEEN

Evolving Ideas About Religion

Doubt isn't the opposite of faith; it is an element of faith.
PAUL TILLICH
AMERICAN THEOLOGIAN

I n his book *God and the American Writer,* Alfred Kazin says he considers religion to be "the most intimate expression of the human heart, . . . the most secret of personal confessions, where we admit to ourselves alone our fears and our losses, our sense of holy dread and our awe before the unflagging power of a universe. . . ."

Do not hesitate to write this chapter if, in your personal spirituality, you are not committed to an organized religion. Unbelief and belief interact in the same arena. You are a contemplative, introspective person who has a relationship with religion. Most people who have chosen not to practice a religion have given earnest thought to their choice. You have a story to write.

～

Change either of these warm-up prompts to be applicable to your life:
- My thoughts about religion are like/different from those of my parents in the following ways . . .
- My religious education/experience . . .

If you decide to read your rough draft aloud to a listener, choose someone who will be sympathetic to your religious perspective, not someone who will wrestle with your ideas. Ask that person to identify the strong features of your writing, and then find out if he has any questions about what you wrote.

If you prefer not to share your experience, read your account aloud to yourself anyway. You'll hear phrases you can improve. Listen to your voice as if you were meeting yourself for the first time.

Important note if you are writing in a fellowship of writers: This time you will have to observe the listeners' guidelines with special strictness so you don't become sidetracked into theological debates. Remember that the purpose of the response group is not to discover absolute truth but to assist the writer in expressing his or her truth. You may need to make extra effort to suspend your own opinions and judgments, listen to learn, and keep the thoughts you heard within the response group.

A writer has just entrusted you with an intimate, important account. Be sensitive to the soul of that writer.

Read aloud your rough drafts and respond to each reader. Say what you admire about the writing. Ask for specific information.

The Reverend John Pierce grew up in the South. An awareness of surroundings that you'll see in this rumination continues throughout his recently written memoirs, "The Sign of the Osprey." Because he now lives in the Pacific Northwest, his current images are of cold rivers, fir trees, and ospreys instead of Spanish moss and bald cypress.

I was raised in a family where each Sunday we went to church. I don't remember religious conversations at the dinner table, yet, like eating breakfast, church was part of the routine.

I was an anomaly. My parents never had to make me go. There was no pressure. Strangely, I wanted to go, yet I never understood all that was going on, only that there was a "presence" there, and I would sit in the pews as though marinating in the juices of the holy. My parents did not quite understand me, for I was drawn to God from my earliest rememberings. I also knew I was different.

My life, like most kids' lives in the subculture of the deep South, consisted of sports and outdoor activities, fishing in the lazy bayous of Louisiana of Spanish moss and bald cypress. From there I knew the mystical properties of low-lying fog skimming the surface of the waters in the early morning light. Fish, snakes, trees, and long-legged cranes spoke to me of the mystery of creation. Even the damp smells of forest and lakes with the sun glistening on surface sparkles of water

*opened my heart to that which I did not comprehend, but which I
would subsequently learn comprehended me. My family gave me root
and an appreciation for beauty and a respect for liturgy, but they
could not answer the intellectual struggles of a youngster. I slipped
into a kind of fundamentalism, trying to put the pieces together of
biblical writ, mystical experiences, and scientific bent of mind and
education. I wanted the definitive in an infinite array of paradoxes.*

*As a student in a university intent on being a doctor, I could not
share what laid claim on me in early life. At the age of three, or
thereabouts, I was baptized. It is one of my earliest remembrances.
In an Episcopal church in downtown Shreveport, Louisiana, I walked
with my parents to the back of the sanctuary and mounted two
wooden steps that elevated me to an appropriate height for the rector
to administer the water. I do not remember the words "I baptize you
in the name of the Father, and the Son, and the Holy Ghost." I only
remember the picture: a small boy, water dripping from his head,
wondering . . . wondering.*

To gather ideas for another chapter, reminisce about the evolution
of your thoughts and feelings about religion with a partner or by yourself. Your experiences may have occurred within a framework of organized religion, or they may have been independent of formal religion.
Make notes as you reminisce.

- From the time when you were growing up, is there a particular
  prayer or verse that you still remember?
- Did certain music used in worship or at other times hold a sacred
  quality for you?
- Did a worship service, such as a particular holiday service, espe-
  cially appeal to you?
- Were religious observances practiced in your home?
- Did a certain place seem especially spiritual to you?
- What people did you know who seemed to have spiritual
  qualities?

If you experienced disillusionment as you grew older, cite instances
of disappointment in:

- people
- institutions
- teachings you believed
- a previous faith

How did these experiences affect your faith?

God does not die on the day when we cease to believe in a personal deity, but we die on the day when our lives cease to be illumined by the steady radiance, renewed daily, of a wonder, the source of which is beyond all reason.

DAG HAMMARSKJÖLD

SECRETARY GENERAL OF THE UNITED NATIONS, RECIPIENT OF THE NOBEL

PEACE PRIZE

Was there a time when you tried to feel the presence of God but could not? What was happening in your life? What were your doubts? Explain your emotions. How has your perception of God changed during your lifetime?

Whether God exists or not remains forever a fascination. But God, believed in or not, remains only the elected Official for the colossal job of mystery. To my mind, prayer was the real question. For prayer exists, no question about that. It is the peculiarly human response to the fact of this endless mystery of bliss and brutality, impersonal might and lyric intimacy that composes our experience of life. As the human response to this mystery, prayer, not the existence of God, is the thing to be decided.

PATRICIA HAMPL

AMERICAN WRITER

This excerpt is from the memoirs of the Reverend Don Purkey, whose childhood religious experience was in a Pentecostal Church in Ohio. When he became a college student at Miami University, he worked during summers in a paper mill. After his marriage he attended a Presbyterian seminary.

I was twelve or thirteen, I can't remember, but I was in the eighth grade when I had two experiences. The first was an evangelist came that was predicting the end of the world. And they always projected a certain date. I remember doing a rough calculation and saying, "Damn it! I won't get through college before He comes."

The other was a traumatic one which has as much influence in causing me to go off in another direction as anything in that period of my life. It was at an evangelistic meeting.

It was incredibly hot, an August night. I can remember the funeral fans that the women held—some of them were paper with pictures of Jesus' life, and others were palm leaf–type things—these rather heavy-bosomed women in their cotton dresses, fanning themselves. And I remember Brother Rose and Sister Bryant and their testimonies.

The evangelist was seventeen to nineteen—I want to say he was seventeen, but it is hard for me to believe that he was still in his teens. He preached on hell, as most of those evangelists were wont to do. He said that if God should send a single bird to earth every million years to pick up one grain of sand, that when the bird had totally removed the whole earth that would be your first split second of burning in hell.

I was traumatized.

It was taken as an indication that I was being saved. I was dragged to the altar and literally thrown on my knees by a surging crowd that was hovering over me with their hands all over me, and I was weeping and crying. I can remember lots of "Praise God" and "Let's pray him through to salvation." It seemed to go on forever and ever. I had been traumatized by what had been said, by the emotional pitch of the service itself, by the physical things happening to me as an adolescent. All of that produced a kind of hysteria that was misunderstood by those who were present.

I came home that night. Inside me I said, "God, if that is the way you are, I'll burn in hell." I cried probably into the morning, finally being so exhausted and falling asleep but having decided sometime during that period that if God was like the God being described, I wanted nothing to do with God. It was an overt kind of decision. I said nothing to anyone but refused from that moment on to go back to church.

You're now used to writing quickly, without hesitation, knowing that you can later expand what you've written, remove portions, rephrase sentences, and rearrange sections. Write about a stage in your religious evolution.

If you're writing with other writers, your time together will limit your development of this subject, but you will succeed in initiating this chapter of your writing.

Hearing what people in your group have written will be not only interesting but suggestive of issues you may want to address. Respond to others' drafts as you always do: Find something positive to say about the writing and ask a question.

No passion in the world is equal to the passion to alter someone else's draft.

H.G. WELLS

WRITER OF SCIENCE FICTION, STUDENT OF POLITICS AND HISTORY

The following paragraphs are part of the memoirs of Aimée Ross-Kilroy. Aimée recently earned her Ph.D. in Renaissance literature and now teaches, mothers her baby daughter, Emma, and enjoys gardening.

I started attending mass again during my senior year of college. Loyola Marymount University had a chapel on campus, and every Advent they followed evening mass with a big tree-lighting ceremony in the quad. So the first Sunday of Advent seemed a good time to start attending church again, after several years away.

It was quite a shock. Apparently some changes had taken place during my absence. I was used to shaking hands with the people around me during the sign of peace. But now I was not only expected to hold hands with people during the Our Father, but I was supposed to watch as "liturgical dancers" wafted down the aisles waving lilac scarves while the offering basket made its rounds. The lights were dimmed and then brightened to heighten the feeling of spectacle as the mass proceeded. I felt a profound sense of displacement.

But in the quiet spaces of the mass I also felt a sense of homecoming. I had tried to "be Buddhist" for a while, but contrary to the beliefs of countless college students like myself, that's a tough thing to do with a paperback book and no community in which to ground yourself. I had felt that the mass had become empty and sterile of meaning, and I was looking for some kind of practice that would connect me daily and deeply to some kind of divinity. So I had stopped attending mass and started reading books.

Now, however, I felt a sense of place and safety. The chapel stretched above me and before me. The light reflected off of the white walls, the wooden stations of the cross. The scent of incense and burning candles was familiar. Like my family, the religion I'd grown up in is weird, dysfunctional even, and often unsatisfactory. But I speak its language and know its terrain. As I held my tiny white taper with its construction paper circle meant to protect my hand from the wax, I marched with all the other students through the cold clear night. Singing in front of the tree in the center of campus, I took a groping baby step toward something I still find difficult to express in words.

～

This is a fine time to sit back, reread all your chapters, and feel pleasure in the quantity and quality of your writing. If you become aware of patterns and relationships in your life that you had not previously noticed, add these observations to your collection of writings.

CHAPTER SEVENTEEN

Confronting Crisis

Out of suffering have emerged the strongest souls; the most massive characters are seared with scars.

E.H. CHAPIN

AMERICAN UNITARIAN MINISTER

Calamitous events test us to the marrow. Our immediate response to distress reveals both our weaknesses and our strengths. Later reflections about our reactions are likely to disclose regrets and good intentions that will never be known beyond ourselves, unless we confide them in our memoirs.

This chapter will help you write about a time when you were tested, a time when you were forced to react to a crisis in your life. The way you would respond to a similar problem now might be different. We don't always look back on past actions as wise or admirable, but we learn with experience. Your response to the crisis will show the person you were then; your reflections will show the person you have become.

If, as you write to one of the following warm-up prompts, you grow warm, if your breath falters, and if you weep, you can be certain you have identified a critical experience about which to write. A writer's physical reactions are a reliable indicator that the subject matter is significant. Commend yourself for narrating a part of your life that may be difficult to write about but is very important to include in your memoirs.

Choose one of these prompts for your first rough draft, or create your own:

- I despaired when . . .
- An agonizing hour for me was when . . .
- I didn't know what to do next or how to go on when . .

Read your rough draft aloud to yourself or to a confidant—or read it silently to yourself. As you listen to it, you're likely to hear phrases you'll want to change. You may also notice that you need to give more background so readers will have a full context in which to understand it.

Important advice for partners and groups: As you listen to the account written by someone else, you may be so caught up in that writer's experience that you will be tempted to give advice, or you may feel an urge to tell about a time when you suffered a worse plight, or you may find that what was catastrophic to the writer seems ordinary to you.

Restrain yourself from evaluating the writer's experience or recounting your own experience. Such commentary will not help the writer achieve candid, frank memoirs. Instead, respond only by recognizing a strength in the writing and asking a question.

Gather ideas for your second draft.

Crises often involve loss. Write notes for yourself about the following kinds of personal loss you have known.

- Loss of a person as a result of
    death
    divorce
    a geographic move
    a mistake
    betrayal
    changes in one or both of you
- Loss of an opportunity
    a relationship
    a career
    a chance for change or growth
    an opportunity missed because you turned away
- Loss of a belief
    in a person
    in a teaching
    in an institution, organization, or profession
    in a religion or philosophy
- Loss of self-control
    toward a person
    while at work
    with drugs or food

- Loss of health
    physical
    mental
    spiritual
- Loss of security or belonging
- Loss of self-confidence or hope

Certain words on your list may seem to pulse with energy. If so, even though you might feel an aversion to the subjects they name, they are likely to be the most powerful and revealing topics you can choose.

⌒

Kathryn Steadman is currently writing a novel as well as devotional materials, poetry, and essays. She is also a Reiki practitioner of hands-on healing.

Kathryn's memoirs tell about a loss she suffered when she was only eight years old—a loss of innocence, a loss of childhood.

The butterman pads down the hallway to my bedroom on his soft, slippery soles. He leaves no imprint on the green shag carpet. The door to my room opens without a sound. He sits on the side of my bed and removes his brown, wing-tip shoes. Was it ten minutes ago or much longer since I knelt on my knees and recited the Our Father?

The porch light shines through the shutters over my window. I begin to count (the butterman puts his finger against my lips, shhh) the slats of light. His fingers smell like pencils.

My legs feel the cool breeze of air as the bedspread is lifted into a tent that the butterman can climb inside. I count the slats backward.

My flannel nightie, the one that began with the red flowers but has faded to pink from so many washings, is pushed to my waist as my panties are pulled down and untangled from around my ankles. I multiply the slats of light two by two.

He pushes against me and I close my eyes to the light. I smell lemon meringue pie on the butterman's breath as he heaves and sighs. I burn as the butterman pours his yellow into me. It hurts forever. It burns a hole into my soul. A hole I build my life around.

When we write about ravaging losses, the opening words are often the most difficult to find. You don't have to start at the beginning of your story. Begin anywhere. You could first describe the scenes that replay themselves in your mind and then later narrate the events that led to those scenes.

Your loss may be personal, or it may encompass your family or community. Poignant memoirs have been written by people exiled from their homes.

Though Chief Joseph was a diplomatic leader who abided by treaties and strove to maintain peace, he and his people were forced off their homeland. At first they did not fight; but later, when war was forced on them, they fought for their freedom. They lost, were captured, and were never allowed to return home.

> It is cold and we have no blankets. The little children are freezing to death. I am tired. My heart is sick and sad. From where the sun now stands, I will fight no more forever.
>
> CHIEF JOSEPH
> HEINMOT TOOYALAKEKT
> NEZ PERCE CHIEF

∽

Rejection brings another kind of crisis. You might begin a draft with these words:

- I felt rejected when . . .

Write rapidly, not pausing to consider what you say. Reflection and revision are best done later.

When you read this draft aloud, listen to it the way a gentle soul mate would listen. Be a compassionate friend to yourself.

We react to crises in many different ways. Fear sometimes causes us to withdraw from others. We may react with anger and defensiveness. To reflect on what you've written, write answers to the following prompts:

- How did you react, and what emotions underlay your reaction?

- Sometimes when a crisis strikes we feel betrayed—by a friend, by a family member, or by God. Tell about any feelings of betrayal you experienced.
- It has been said that the human condition is to betray and to be betrayed. If in your crisis you betrayed someone else or yourself, explain how that was so.
- Another facet of the human condition is the longing for reconciliation. Did you find reconciliation with a person, with yourself, with God?
- Sometimes forgiveness is involved. If forgiveness is part of the story of your crisis, tell how you forgave or were forgiven or have been unable to forgive.
- You may have accepted your loss, or you may not have become resigned to it. How do you feel about it now?
- If you have come to see your loss as leading to gain and do not now regret it, explain how this is so.

Reread your story, looking for the following underlying qualities in yourself and in others. Write paragraphs about how you find these qualities manifested or absent:
- faith
- compassion
- generoslty
- hope
- resolve

⌐

The memoirs of Jan Adams relate a time when her husband, Jack, was caught in an impossible career predicament. A New York agency hired him as director at the same time it implemented "key limitations in personnel and finance" and reduced his assistant's salary. She left, leaving Jack to try to untangle insoluble problems.

My easily spouted philosophy that "people can be happy anywhere as long as they get into a community and make friends" was crum-

bling. It's not easy to "fit in" when you're struggling with overwhelming circumstances. Even the church seemed filled with successful people while our own discouragement caused us to feel awkward and out of place. I remember fondly the Russells, a caring couple who reached out to us and still remind me (through a little glass ladybug they gave to us) to "never underestimate the power of a simple kindness."

We went to parks—talking, walking, and sharing our search for solutions. I developed a dislike for ducks, which were plentiful in these locations and somehow became a symbol for me of hopelessness. (I have since grown to appreciate them on the lake where we happily settled in retirement.) None of my newly acquired counseling skills seemed to work for me. I remember telling a Eugene friend that we were trapped and had no choices. She unsympathetically replied, "You'd better find some." True, but difficult under the circumstances. I realized how "misplaced" I felt when a trip to J.C. Penney made me homesick! Or when I took our Christmas letter to a copy shop to have the employee look at it and ask, "You're from Oregon? And you left? Why?" That echoed my sentiment as my dream of a grand new adventure dissolved into a nightmare.

In October I withdrew from the Blanton-Peale Institute and moved into job-searching mode, not my favorite activity. After discouraging possibilities (long hours, low pay), I received a call from Phyllis Jean Rodgers, Jack's cousin who was a high school counselor in New Jersey and who had heard of an opening in Edison. I protested that I couldn't do that because I'd never worked with high school students. P.J.'s unsympathetic response, "You've got transferable skills. Go for it!" So that was the risk that Jack's desperation pushed me to take, leading to a happy discovery and a wonderful career opportunity for me in future years.

. . . Jack was able to quit his job and gradually recover from the trauma of that pressure.

CHAPTER EIGHTEEN

Longings

Prayer is not asking. It is a longing of the soul.

MAHATMA GANDHI
SPIRITUAL AND POLITICAL LEADER OF INDIA

When we respond to a work of art—a passage of literature, a painting, a photograph, or a strain of music—we create a tie that connects us. At one end is the work of art; at the other end is a place in our souls. The reaction to a poem or a prayer is about the person who reads it or prays it, as well as about the poem or prayer. When we explain why a particular selection is meaningful, our explications are partly about the object and partly about ourselves.

This chapter will guide you in writing about what it is in you that responds to a work of art or an object, as well as about the work itself.

> If you are writing with a partner or fellowship of writers, bring your selection to your gathering. It could be something from one of the following categories or from outside these categories:
> - prayer
> - poem
> - selection of music
> - passage of literature
> - work of art
> - familial blessing

To start the flow of words and ideas, write spontaneously about a time when you felt a strong emotion. You may choose any emotion, such as grief, fear, relief, bliss, exhilaration, compassion, remorse, anger, outrage, love, pity, despair, or determination.

Begin with the following prompt:
- A time when I felt intense . . . was when . . .

When you read aloud this rough draft, imagine that the best friend you ever had is beside you, listening.

> This prompt could lead you into passageways of your life where you experienced extreme distress. These are the times when we fervently seek understanding and reassurance. To read aloud about these experiences may cause the voice to quiver. To recall one's emotion can trigger tears. If you are able to share your story with two or three people, your writing will benefit from their responses; however, this time you may prefer to read what you've written to a single listener.
>
> What should you do if someone in your writing group cries—or if you do? First, realize that the writer has succeeded in identifying and writing about a meaningful experience. Commend the writer for having the courage to explore a significant issue. Pass the tissues, and share the emotion in an accepting, sympathetic, nonjudgmental manner. Keep in mind that you'll say nothing about the writing outside of your group, and proceed to respond as usual.

Memoirs are written in the narrative genre, but they can include your poetry, letters, journal entries, essays, and prayers.

When Lisa Rosen wrote about her longing for a child, her writing took the form of a poem. Lisa is a writer who lives with her husband, Don, and dog, Orion, in a charming house where the garden has recently sprouted thimbleberries.

Sarah Speaks

For years I ran with my heart
to a place that took me close to ground
close to the cool smell of clay.

Across the river
was a dream
printed in topaz
and in that bee-gold glow
where every seed that longs for form
is granted abundant body,
one of me walks with my own young son.

And everywhere his small fingers
are touching happiness.
He's fanning them to feel
the pattering sift
of tumbling pebbles,
he's sweeping them through the air
to point at birds,
he's clasping his fig cake
and reaching for me.

Watching, but marooned
and barren,
I would practice letting go.
I had only to soften my fists
to understand surrender.
I could unfurl my fingers
balled dense as tree burls
and little by little, let
the exhausted reach
of my heart relax.

Little by little I stopped counting moons,
stopped drizzling pomegranate seeds
into my supper cup. I bent toward
the small face that made a family
of Abraham's face and mine, and said good-bye.

With empty arms, I got up
and began walking the slow mountain
of forgiveness toward Hagar.
Ages later, when that traveler
came stroking the frayed thread
of my old prayers,
naturally I laughed
thinking of the brittle rind
my body had become.

Is anything too difficult
for the Lord? he asked sharply.
I knew it was
the sizzling voice of God.

I grew hot and small
as girlhood then
and fear gushed from me
in a lie: I didn't laugh.
Ah, he said, but you did.

If you are writing independently, take time now to reflect on the draft you've just written. If you are with other writers, put the following suggestions aside to reflect on and write about at a later time, before you revise this rough draft.

- Ponder where in your account you reveal the quality of tenderness in yourself and the quality of patience.
- What was your source of courage?
- Where did you find hope?
- How were the hidden parts of yourself affected?

Now you are ready to write about the object you identified as meaningful to you. Your writing will flow more readily if you first tell a friend or writing partner about the art or craft you have selected. In the same way that small children automatically and naturally learn to talk before they learn to write, experienced adult writers verbalize mentally before writing. If we've been composing silently while doing chores and tasks, that preparation enables us to commence writing without hesitation when we sit down at our desks. Speaking aloud to someone is even more effective than composing silently because the presence of a listener gives awareness of how our sentences are working and where further explanation is needed. First, read, show, play, or sing whatever you selected. Then tell:

- what was happening in your life when you were drawn to your selection
- what you interpret it as saying or expressing

- what emotions or attitudes you relate to in the selection
- what this selection reflects about yourself
- how your life has been affected by experiencing the selection

Dare to ramble as you write your rough draft. In as much as you have prepared to write by speaking, you already know what you intend to say and how you'll say it, but what you say unexpectedly will produce insights, so allow unplanned thoughts to emerge. They're more likely to flash from your subconscious if you write speedily, without forethought.

⌐

A prayer by Marianne Williamson has been especially meaningful to Adrienne Lannom, who created fifteen homes that she shared with her first and second husbands, four children, and six grandchildren. Adrienne is a retired researcher and editor.

Here are two lines from the prayer and Adrienne's reflections:

"may we all be blessed;
may we find our way home. . . ."
What I know intuitively as "home" has often appeared in dreams at critical times in my life. Even in its various dream guises, I have always recognized it as the place of my earliest memories of myself.

I remember my home—my "real" home—the one I reach back to and search for in corners and closets and dresser drawers.

My mother tells me we will leave it and move to a bigger home in a better place far away. I was nine. At least I feel nine in the memory, although accuracy would demand that I say I was a year beyond that. It was in the spring of 1944.

I begged her to let me stay there—in that two-family house we shared with my cousins and aunt and uncle. I remember lying on the daybed in the dining room under the picture of God. That I believed it was a picture of God would've been a surprise to Mom and Pop, if they'd known. I have no idea what happened to that picture. I don't remember seeing it in the new house or anywhere again. . . .

I became lonely and homeless for the first of many times. I learned to be alone and to search for home. As I grew up and was on my own, I made and remade new nests and found or was given others to share them with me. But then I didn't find new friends, not like the ones I loved most, the ones who sustained me, the ones I'd lost— Evie, Lucy, Tomy, Louis, Billy, Tessie. It was a big step up from the familiar Italian-Irish neighborhood in Queens to Riverdale and the Upper Westside of New York. Only I never left Queens. It was real, it was me. It loved and nurtured and comforted me. It let me be who I was without comment or criticism. It let me fit comfortably in my own skin. It didn't push to change me, to make me grow and compete for my place. It let me live with sorrow and birth and death, without fear. It stayed hidden deep within me, so deeply I often forgot it was there, but I dreamed it alive many times.

When I need to find me, that's where I am. In the patch of lawn near the garage in the backyard—Auntie's clothesline edging the paved driveway. The sun heating the brick walls and the back stoop where my cousin and I dried our hair on Saturday afternoons— mine primly braided to tame it, Evie's rolled with rags to curl it for Sunday mass at St. Joan of Arc's. Uncle Frank in the downstairs kitchen cutting the boys' hair, and occasionally the girls', the Met broadcast or an Italian-language station playing opera recordings loud enough to discourage conversation or mute the sounds of disagreement. The five blue stars on the banner in the front window for the sons and husbands "in the war." My cousin Louise, ill and slowly dying in the big bed in her parents' room by the window that overlooked the yard and caught the morning sun, her sister Lucy angrily scolding Evie and me for forgetting her suffering and letting the back door slam as we chased through the house and up the stairs, rounding up brothers and cousins for a game of ball or king of the hill in the vacant lot behind the house on a summer afternoon.

If you're writing independently, ask a trusted friend to listen, or just read your rough draft aloud to yourself in a comfortable, private setting.

Take notes as you reflect on this rough draft. Write about any ways your experience with your subject brought about:

- transcendence
- illumination
- energy
- serenity
- reverence
- resolution
- compassion
- spiritual presence

Memoirists sometimes ask how they'll know when they have revised their rough drafts enough. Occasionally a draft seems right without any revision. Sometimes we make a few changes and get a feeling of "there!" Many people revise and revise until they sense it is right. For more information, see chapter twenty-nine.

⌒

The two chapters you have just completed have brought you yet closer to the center of your spiritual labyrinth.

One must not lose desires. They are mighty stimulants to creativeness, to love and to long life.
DR. ALEXANDER BOGOMOLETS
DEPARTMENT OF PATHOLOGIC PHYSIOLOGY, SECOND MOSCOW
UNIVERSITY

If you are writing with fellow writers, plan a celebratory gathering at which each participant will read one chapter, not to exceed a set length of time. Remind everyone to observe the guidelines for good listening and responding. Pass cake and fruit, and savor a feast of words and sweets.

CHAPTER NINETEEN

Love

He who loves feels love descend into him and if he has wisdom, may
perceive it is from the Poetic Genius, which is the Lord.
WILLIAM BLAKE
ENGLISH POET AND PAINTER

Love is a great mystery. In all its guises—altruistic, familial, erotic,
and communal—it brings joy into our lives. When our offer of love
is rejected, we wince, we may bleed emotionally, and we sometimes
grow thick, protective scars. When love fades away, our souls become
dusty and dry.

We cannot concoct or contrive love. It is a gift. We can create
opportunities for love to appear, and we can nurture the conditions in
which love thrives, but ultimately love comes or it does not. We are
blessed or not.

~

As you write this chapter you'll remember the times when love kin-
dled your being. Such times may be fleeting or enduring, but always
they are tender and sweet.

I was dead and now I am alive.
I was in tears and now I am laughing
The power of love swept over my soul
    and now I am that eternal power.
JELALUDDIN RUMI
TURKISH SUFI POET, THIRTEENTH CENTURY

The love we received in infancy prepared us to form emotional bonds
and enabled us to become empathetic people. Our essential first experiences of love occurred when we were very young.

Most of us sensed that we were loved, whether by a parent, grandparent, or someone else. To initiate your thoughts and words on the subject of love, write quickly and spontaneously about the person who loved you when you were a child and how that love was expressed.

- As a child I received love . . .

If you were not loved, then write about that circumstance.

Love is patient and kind; love is not jealous or boastful; it is not arrogant or rude. Love does not insist on its own way; it is not irritable or resentful; it does not rejoice at wrong but rejoices in the right. Love bears all things, believes all things, hopes all things, endures all things.

I CORINTHIANS 13:4–7
THE BIBLE

Read aloud your rough draft singly or with other writers.

〜

Gather ideas before you begin your second writing on the subject of love. On a large sheet of paper, name some objects of your love as you were growing up. Of course, you may name more than one—or none.

- a pet
- an adult
- a classmate or friend
- an idol
- a teenager or young adult
- another person you have loved

〜

The following selection is by Joan Pierson, a Presbyterian minister and a spiritual director. Earlier she taught comparative literature and English at the University of Oregon.

Twice I have been sick with love, and twice people have been sick with love for me. I speak of four people here, not two, and this arithmetic says something about the strange and bitter asymmetries of loving.

I learned early about the vicissitudes of love. When I was four I went to a little preschool at a neighbor's house. Each morning my mother would take my hand and walk with me one block uphill and then, turning to the right, half another block and across the street to Vera's, and there she would leave me with half a dozen little girls and four little boys.

One of the boys was Ralphie, and he loved me. I still had my long golden curls and the assurance that I was very lovable. Ralphie would offer up most of his snack to me. He shared with me books and toys, and more than once snatched from another child a toy I coveted and put it in my hand. I never had to ask. By some strange alchemy of love he simply understood what would please me.

In the middle of that year I became quite ill with infected ears, a common childhood happening in those days before sulfa and penicillin. The doctor came with his black case and took from it a horrendous needle, with which he lanced my ears. I remember struggle, tears, screams even, followed by an abrupt end to pain and many comforts— attention, ice cream, new games and toys.

The illness went on for days, with unpleasant visits from the doctor and daily dosings with bitter medicine—mouth, nose, and ears. And then one day, Ralphie, who missed me, longed for me, came to visit. His father brought him, and he carried, wrapped in toilet paper, his favorite toy, a nearly new red fire engine.

How lovely, how generous. But, at the very moment Marie let them in the front door, a life-changing mishap occurred. My mother, in her haste to get downstairs to greet our company, made a mistake in the medication she was giving me. Into my ears went a stopperful of nose drops—no damage done. But, up my nose went the fiercely potent eardrops. My head was afire. I screamed and screamed. And Ralphie, downstairs, bolted for the door, followed by his apologetic father. He dropped the fire truck, and later my little brother loved it.

Eventually I returned to Vera's preschool. Ralphie was still there, but he avoided me all the days till summer came and his family moved to another neighborhood. And so I learned very young that

*love, that powerful emotion, is also fragile and can disappear forever
when it is too hard pressed.*

⟿

Sometimes our love is never revealed. Quietly we pulse with the
pleasure and the pain of unexpressed love. Make another list, written
or mental, of the people you have loved in this way.

At Last

You have come
and you did well to come
I pined for you.
And now you have put a torch to my heart
a flare of love—
O bless you and bless you and bless you:
you are back . . .
we were parted

> SAPPHO
> GREEK LYRIC POET, BORN C. 615 B.C.

Immerse yourself in memories as you write a rough draft about a
time when your love was strong. Look for the uniqueness of your experience. Love pays little heed to prescribed rules. It may flame in our
hearts for people forbidden to us by social norms. It may violate the
conventions of eligible or heterosexual coupling—yet it is undeniable.
You may decide whether or not to share the rough draft you're about
to write with listeners. For the moment, write candidly. If you decide
to withhold this selection from friends or fellow writers, feel free to say
simply, "I pass."

Remember a time when you felt intense, overwhelming love. Write
about how you met your beloved and about your increasing emotion.
Your story may describe both spiritual and sexual feelings, feelings of
longing and of unity.

⟿

Though the boy mentioned here noticed me only once and spoke a single sentence to me during a week at camp, I still remember him and the way I felt.

> *We were at church camp in the mountains, where the pine-strained wind was so dry and cold it pricked our nostrils. In a corner of the mess hall, away from the clatter of dinner dishwashing and the whoops of boys in a game of chase, Sydney played the piano. He was older than I. Tall. Chocolate brown hair. A manly chest. An inviting grin.*
>
> *I stood with other kids gathered around the piano and watched his large hands shape the chords as we sang hymns of hope and love, "Breathe on me, breath of God. Fill me with life anew," and my chest expanded with the swelling of the songs until prickles showered down my back. Our voices braided into tones that tightened my throat with sweet longing, longing for God, longing for him. I closed my eyes and imagined kneeling beside him, drinking from the chalice his lips had touched, swallowing God's gift—and I yearned.*

If you are still with the person you loved intensely, you may enjoy reading this rough draft to him or her. If you are no longer with that person, slowly read aloud your account, recalling the sensations you felt. Consider reading this remembrance to a dear friend.

Advice to listeners: Set aside conventional expectations about love, and open your hearts to new possibilities and truths. Real life often deviates from the plots of romance novels, and we do not always follow the advice of our elders. Avoid judgmental thoughts, listen to learn, comment on the strength of the writing, and ask questions that will help the writer render a full, rich account.

Pat Vallerand did not expect love to enter her life in the way it did.

If you are writing with a partner or group of writers, you probably have a sense of whether your fellow writers will be sympathetic or might condemn your feelings. We do become vulnerable when we confide powerful feelings. If your listeners are respectful, read this draft to them.

This part of her memoirs shows the unpredictability of love.

Pat continues to be devoted to and live happily with her partner of thirty years.

Something very strange was happening here. Something completely out of my control.

I was confused. But I did know that my feelings were intense—a deep, fervent, yet reverent feeling of love and longing. Different than any love or longing I had ever experienced before. As if my soul were waking up to a gift from the divine.

Cheryl and I had met at the First Baptist Church when I was attending the university and was new to town. My background was quite different from hers. She had grown up in that church, her father was a well-respected local banker, her mother the church organist. I had grown up in the Catholic Church in Lewiston, Maine, a French Canadian with parents who were working-class immigrants. I noticed her immediately. I think what drew me to her was her sense of assurance. But not an egotistical kind of assurance. An assurance that was grounded and open.

She was intelligent and had an incredible sense of humor—an understated way of seeing the absurd in most everything. She reached out in a selfless, loving way to others that I could not help but admire. She was particularly drawn to reach out to those who others tended to overlook.

We had both signed up to accompany the church's youth group which was traveling by train to attend a national Youth for Christ Conference in Illinois. Through a strange series of events, we both ended up traveling separately from the church group, arriving in Urbana ahead of them, by plane, me from California and Cheryl from Portland. Alone and somewhat anxious in this new setting, I spied Cheryl across a large auditorium of thousands of people and became her roommate for the duration of the four-day conference.

It is still hard for me to describe what happened during those four days. But in that atmosphere of love and divine power, I knew that I had found a soul mate. A friend like no other.

Talk was the thread that wove the friendship together. We spoke about everything that was important to us—our lives and spiritual goals. I had never felt so comfortable talking about these intimate subjects with anyone before. No matter what I said, she seemed to accept me—a truly new experience for me. She continued to amaze me with her intelligence, humor, and caring, and I also came to see the depths of her spiritual grounding.

When we returned from the conference, we cherished and nourished this newfound friendship. I was living on campus. Cheryl, who was also attending the university, was living at home with her parents. But we didn't let that impede our progress! We made time to meet to continue our talks.

I knew my feelings for Cheryl were intense, but I did not realize how intense until one day when I was sitting in the living room of my cooperative house with a housemate, Mary, and saw Cheryl walking toward the house to join me for lunch. Mary, whose back was to the window, stopped the conversation by saying, "I guess Cheryl is here." I jumped and said, "How do you know?" Her reply came with a smirk, "It's obvious from the look on your face."

The comment stunned me, but I put it out of my mind for the time being. This was 1970 after all. I had no understanding of what it meant to fall in love with another woman. But fall in love I did.

It became clear to me that Cheryl's feelings were as strong as mine. But we didn't have any idea what to do with those feelings. For a time, we channeled them all into those endless talks. Hours of talking. We met between classes and talked. We skipped classes and talked. We called each other on the phone and talked. We met at church and talked.

All of this intercourse resulted inevitably in sharing deep and painful issues for both of us. Of course, discussing hurts and traumas led us to a strong desire to provide comfort—both emotional, and, as we grew closer, physical—the physical comfort we had both been deprived of growing up in our families.

When Cheryl spoke to me about the hurts in her life, I felt them as strongly as she did. I ached and cried with her. She ached and cried with me. And, finally, we held each other in a deep, passionate, loving embrace. Oh, what a feeling. What a sense of arriving—

arriving home. Arriving to something sacred and complete.

～

Respond in writing to the following questions for reflection. Some of the answers you write are likely to develop into paragraphs that you'll integrate into your draft.

- What does the love you felt show about yourself?
- Did you intuitively know something about your beloved?
- Did you sense a vitalizing principle or sacred presence?
- What did your relationship mean in the overview of your life?

A Smile and a Gentleness

There is a smile and a gentleness
inside. When I learned the name

and address of that, I went to where
you sell perfume. I begged you not

to trouble me so with longing. Come
out and play! Flirt more naturally.

Teach me how to kiss. On the ground
a spread blanket, flame that's caught

and burning well, cumin seeds browning,
I am inside all this with my soul.

    JELALUDDIN RUMI
    TURKISH SUFI POET, THIRTEENTH CENTURY

Not everyone has experienced a loving marriage or partnership. If your attempts to find a mate have been unsatisfactory, write about your expectations and your disappointment. If you found fulfillment in other ways, write about the close, supportive relationships you've had with particular friends, colleagues, or children.

About your rich and satisfying union, list:
- the ways you complemented each other
- pleasures shared
- what you most appreciate about your beloved
- mutual achievements
- how you've supported each other through difficulties
- the source of resilience in your relationship
- feelings of devotion or compassion
- what enabled you to transcend times of stress or dissatisfaction
- a time or times when you seemed to be in a world of your own

Love does not consist in gazing at each other but in looking outward together in the same direction.
ANTOINE DE SAINT-EXUPÉRY
FRENCH AVIATOR AND WRITER

To edit your draft, look to see if you've described your beloved. Facts about size, coloring, and dress are less important than the impressions you had of that person.

Quotations add life and individuality to descriptions of people. If you can remember something the person once said or used to say, insert it.

Descriptions of typical reactions also help readers know a person. How did your beloved show anger? Worry? Happiness? What caused him or her to feel those emotions?

If these specific suggestions seem to fit into your writing, describe habitual gestures, the sound of the voice, and the way your beloved moved.

As you describe an experience you shared, describe yourself, too. Tell how you felt both physically and emotionally.

What qualities in yourself were enhanced by your relationship with your beloved?

Did the love you shared give you a sense of something larger than yourselves?

Was there a time when you felt your love to be sacred? Holy?

When you write your final draft, leave space for photographs of the people and animals you have loved.

And one of His signs is that He created for you spouses from your own selves so that you find tranquillity with them, and He creates the love and mercy between you. Therein are certainly signs for people who think about things.

QURAN 30:21

THE SACRED BOOK OF MUSLIMS

CHAPTER TWENTY
Flip of the Compass

As Gregor Samsa awoke one morning from uneasy dreams he found
himself transformed in his bed into a gigantic insect. He was lying on his
hard, as it were armor-plated, back and when he lifted his head a little
he could see his domelike brown belly divided into stiff arched segments
on top of which the bed quilt could hardly keep in position and was
about to slide off completely. His numerous legs, which were pitifully
thin compared to the rest of his bulk, waved helplessly before his eyes.
What has happened to me? . . . It was no dream.
    FRANZ KAFKA
    GERMAN NOVELIST

Like Gregor Samsa, many of us have awakened to new and disorient-
ing realizations. The familiar, safe life we took for granted shifted
into a new landscape until even the bedrock under our homes cracked.
The points of the compass that had always indicated security and right-
ness quivered, off course.

Profound disruptions occur and disorient us at any age: A parent
departs, someone we love becomes alcoholic or mentally ill or abusive,
a trusted spouse prefers someone else, we are stricken with illness, someone we love dies.

The disruption is not always negative. We get a lucky break. A
scholarship opens doors into a new world. We find ourselves in an
unexpected career, living a different lifestyle. We discover we have aptitudes or talents or callings we didn't know we had. We realize we aren't
the person our parents hoped we would be—or the person we thought
we were. We discover a letter that reveals a new way of understanding
a relationship. We see why someone did what he did. We learn a secret.
We see the world differently.

The Cyclone had set the house down, very gently—for a cyclone—in
the midst of a country of marvelous beauty. There were lovely patches

of green sward all about, with stately trees bearing rich and luscious fruits. Banks of gorgeous flowers were on every hand, and birds with rare and brilliant plumage sang and fluttered in the trees and bushes. A little way off was a small brook, rushing and sparkling along between green banks, and murmuring in a voice very grateful to a little girl who had lived so long on the dry, gray prairies.

L. FRANK BAUM

AMERICAN CHILDREN'S AUTHOR

Soon you're going to write about a time in your life when you faced unexpected circumstances and had to relinquish your earlier assumptions, but first, warm up to writing. Choose one of the following four prompts.

> **If you're writing with other writers, tell a partner how you anticipate writing to one of these prompts.**

- In my family, we never talked about . . .
- We talked about . . . only when . . . was not present.
- I didn't learn about . . . until I was . . .
- When we talked about . . . the words we used were . . .

Note: Certain subjects are sometimes taboo—a reprehensible relative, money, sex, cancer, someone's earlier life, AIDS, and other topics. The banned subjects are often of major importance. If they were not considered threatening, then they could be discussed casually; it's because they are loaded with implications that they must be squelched. The dynamics of our families cannot be understood without identifying the dangers indicated by the silenced subjects. As a writer reminiscing about your family, you may now speak about what was unspoken.

A milder form of censorship is restriction of vocabulary. Euphemisms are often substituted when direct speech seems harshly illuminating. Euphemisms are often selected for aesthetic reasons. Another form of restriction occurs when certain subjects are discussed but only under guarded conditions, behind closed doors, or among only particular family members. This in itself is interesting.

If your family talked freely about everything, then write about the liberation and lack of censorship in your family; if your family always seemed to talk about the same thing, tell about that.

Write for about fifteen minutes, and then share your draft with a friend, a relative, or fellow writers. Ask your friend or listeners to respond by first indicating what they like about your writing and then asking a question about something you didn't tell.

⌒

Marlene Elam Neal grew up in Westfir, a tiny picturesque town nestled under fir trees in the Cascade Mountains. As a young mother she traveled and lived in other places, but at this time she again lives near her childhood community. She teaches a Bible class to four-year-olds.

> *In my family we never talked about religion. It wasn't until I was almost adult that I gained a clue as to why not. My mother had been raised very strict German Lutheran while my father's family had leaned toward Christian Science. I had been baptized as a baby in the Lutheran Church, but since I grew up in a small mill town I had always gone to Sunday School at a community church. It started out Baptist but was Presbyterian by the time I was in my junior high years. Dad later became a Mason, so the only disparaging remarks I ever heard were against the Roman Catholic Church, which I was somehow led to believe was all wrong, and I became very proud to put down Protestant whenever called upon to fill in a blank that said religion. It now reminds me of a friend's teenager who, when asked by some girls if he was a Christian, replied, "No. I'm a Baptist."*

⌒

Do you already know the subject of your second draft? You may readily identify a time when your assumptions and expectations about your life fundamentally shifted. If so, you know what you'll write about. Many people think of a time when a relationship with a person changed. A woman in a workshop wrote about her discovery that her older sister was really her mother. Realizations even less astonishing jar one's personal view of the world.

Your life may have taken an unexpected turn when something you could not anticipate interfered with your plans—or provided opportunities. You might have found yourself living in a new place where the rules and expectations were different. The money you relied on could have ceased. Someone you adored or emulated disillusioned you. Your employer or some other authority did something surprising. A new person assumed the role of authority. A belief you held became implausible.

The reorientation could have come from within yourself as you grew to know yourself better. A teenage writer wondered why he dreamed of boys, not of girls. Talents and aptitudes may emerge. An aspiring actor realized he could succeed in a career on stage but would live far from home and lose the sense of community he shared with his rural, farm family. Conversely, we often become aware that we do not have sufficient aptitude to fulfill long-held dreams. These sorts of recognitions destabilize us. The compass swings wildly. We have to reorient ourselves.

⌐

John A. Callahan, a chemical microscopist, has developed analytical instruments to control air and water emissions at industrial plants such as pulp mills. His pleasures are clog dancing and singing and acting with a troupe that performs in public schools.

This part of his memoirs tells how his life suddenly changed.

> *A difficult time was when I came home from work, and my wife was not there. My younger daughter told me that she had gone to the local junior college to practice her typing. . . . My wife suffered from mental problems and her actions were not always predictable. She would often go for long walks with the dog, and I didn't know when to expect her home.*
>
> *When it got dark, I began to worry about her. I called my married daughter and asked if her mother was there. She said that she had been, but she left. My wife was gone all night. She wasn't home by the time I had to go to work the next day. When I got home that*

evening, it appeared as if she had been in the house during the day, but she wasn't home. I went to her typing class, hoping that she would be there. She wasn't. I checked all the places and people that might know anything about her. I found out nothing. I could tell, though, that she had been in the house during the day. She was just avoiding us. However, my life had to go on. I still had four kids living at home. It wasn't easy. I was concerned for her welfare but was powerless to do anything about it.

～

If you have not already discerned your subject for this writing, then name:

- A shift in relationships that surprised you
    familial
    among friends
    with people at work
    a change in physical well-being
    an unexpected disability
    an enabling achievement
    a death
- Times when circumstances changed your mind-set
    a new place
    an opportunity lost or gained
    sudden hardship or affluence
    a surprising change in yourself
    revolutionary ideas
    a new role
    a shift in values

I know well what I am fleeing from but not what I am in search of.
   MICHEL DE MONTAIGNE
   FRENCH ESSAYIST

Because you're writing about a major change in your life, this topic is likely to require more time to narrate than previous subjects have taken. Throughout the coming days you can add to your quick first draft by adding background to show your life before the change and to explain the impact of the shift on the rest of your life. At this time, write about the particular event of your realization.

An easy way to begin is with the words, "I was. . . ." If you are writing in a fellowship of writers, give yourself at least thirty minutes to initiate this draft.

After working as a paralegal/investigator for many years, Cheryl Roffe left the legal field to pursue what she says is a simpler, healthier lifestyle more congruent with her spiritual values. She is now a volunteer mediator with a nonprofit community mediation agency and a photo archivist in a historical museum.

My world disintegrated in a single day, August 11, 1970. It was my only day off from the cannery where I worked during the summer to earn money for my college tuition. I was nineteen years old and a devout Christian whose goal in life was to find a career where I could be of service and provide healing to a suffering world. I'd always excelled at what my family considered the important things—academics, handling duties and obligations, being an exemplary "Christian" girl. I'd always been "on track," in spite of the periodic questions and doubts that had been surfacing in my mind since I was nine or ten years old.

Well I certainly got off track on this particular day—in fact, I derailed dramatically and decisively. The day started calmly enough; I remember sitting in the living room painting an oil paint-by-number scene of a mountain landscape and listening to music on the radio. I was alone and felt very peaceful.

Suddenly, out of nowhere (or so it seemed to me) came the thought, "F--- God!" I was stunned and horrified. To use such a word, and in connection with God, too! It was certainly not a word I used in everyday life, nor did anyone I associated with use it. I thought I'd committed the unforgivable sin that the preachers kept warning us about—blasphemy of the Holy Spirit. I tried to erase the obscene words, but the more I tried, the worse it got—those two words repeating themselves over and over again in my brain, louder and louder and louder.

In a matter of moments, the structure on which I'd built my nineteen years of life was shattered. For I believed that if I could think such a thought, I could not be what I thought I was. I could not be a Christian, I could not be a respectable person, I could not help others because I was in dire need of help myself. No one who was worth anything could have ever thought such a thought, I was sure.

All day long, the inner war continued. By the time I went to the cannery to work the night shift, I was completely lost in nightmares. The words had expanded into images—visions of violence and sex and all the taboo things that I had never thought of before, or at least, had never been aware of thinking about.

I had known there was evil in the world—we heard about that constantly in church. But I had never dreamed that so much of that evil was in me, as well. I was shocked, devastated, and shamed to the core, and I had absolutely no idea what was happening to me or what I could do about it. I couldn't believe that someone who read the Bible and prayed every day could be seeing and thinking what I was seeing and thinking. Certainly no one I had ever talked with or heard speak at home or at church had ever mentioned anything like this.

When lunchtime came at midnight, I was desperate enough that I had to do something. I had always kept my private affairs to myself— I did not even discuss them with my family. But this was too overwhelming—I was terrified that I was going crazy, or worse. So I called home. My father answered the phone. I couldn't explain what was happening to me—I hardly knew myself—and I could not articulate the ugly, revolting things that were going through my mind. So I simply asked him to help me because "the Devil was trying to take over my mind."

Cheryl has shown us the particular day when her life lost its moorings. Her dramatic depiction prepares us for further narration about a spiritual struggle during young adulthood and an eventual reorientation. Like Cheryl's draft, the one you have just written is also likely to function as an opening for a longer chapter. Your readers will want to know how you coped with your disorientation and what impact it made on your life.

⌐

Read your rough draft aloud to yourself or to listeners. If upon hearing it you would like to revise it to be more vivid and to convey a sense of immediacy and presence, review chapter four.

Write reflective paragraphs in answer to the following questions:

- What were your fears?
- If you prayed, what was your prayer?
- How did you direct your anger?
- Throughout the time of reorientation, whom or what did you trust?
- What gave you your sources of self-confidence?
- Where did you find the energy to do what you needed to do?
- How did your beliefs or assumptions change?
- What resulting good, if any, came from the "flip in your compass"?
- How have you now reconciled your feelings about the experience?
- What dimensions in yourself did your reorientation reveal?

How true it is that what we really see day by day depends less on the objects and scenes before our eyes than on the eyes themselves and the minds and hearts that use them.

FREDERIC DAN HUNTINGTON
FIRST EPISCOPAL BISHOP, NEW YORK

You're now ready to revise your rough draft. Add to it, change it, rearrange it, or, if it's already the way you want it to be, leave it as it is.

Read aloud your revised rough draft once more before having it proofread and writing your final draft.

⌐

It's possible that the kind of writing you have just completed would fall into a literary category called "coming of age" or "rite of passage." Such writings are usually about the loss of innocence. The main character emerges from one world into another where she or he may confront evil or have to accept disappointment or disillusionment. Novels reflecting this theme are often about adolescents, but rites of passage continue to occur as long as we confront destabilizing changes.

CHAPTER TWENTY-ONE

Inner Peace

Calm Soul of all things! make it mine
To feel, amid the city's jar,
That there abides a peace of thine,
Man did not make, and can not mar.
  MATTHEW ARNOLD
  ENGLISH POET AND CRITIC

The human condition encompasses both peace and turmoil; they are interwoven through our psyches. A complex mix of external and internal factors determines our vulnerability to distress and our ability to find peace. Many of us teeter between a place of inner calm and a tendency to fret, so we are grateful for periods of repose.

To write better about the times and the conditions in which our souls find peace, we must also acknowledge and consider the episodes when our feelings war against other people, toward the world in general, and even against ourselves. You'll first write about causes of turbulence in your life and then about how you find peace.

This writing, by a woman who does not want members of her family to identify its author, shows how the characteristics of her husband tarnished her inner peace.

Jerry's moods are the motivating factors of his life, and during our marriage I set about the business of trying to "positivize" his moods by giving him what he wanted. His predominant mood is that of a soldier waiting for an ambush. A year in Vietnam as well as his violent upbringing gives him the sense that the world is always out to "get" him. He is ready to fight at the least provocation and if none should appear, he creates one to fill his need. Even when he tries to relax in the evenings by watching TV, his loud, voracious fingernail biting is a sign that his guard is never over. He is combat ready.

Jerry's soul seeks satisfaction in ownership. He insisted that we live in the country because neighbors are untrustworthy pests, so we bought a small farm. He accumulates every implement ever heard of by the mechanical-minded farmer. Tractors, trailers, hay mowers, balers, grain grinders, plows . . . he has to have them all! Every time he has an idea for a new piece of machinery he obsesses over it, pores over the classified ads, travels thousands of miles, until he eventually purchases what he wants. Nothing really makes Jerry happy because rust corrodes even the most sophisticated of machinery.

Jerry doesn't take kindly to anyone who gets in the way of him and something he wants. He walks determinedly in his boots, threatening, attacking, and defeating anyone who tries to stand in his way. He knows how to get what he wants. In my visual image of Jerry, he's wearing grease-stained, work-worn logger jeans held up with a pair of wide, stretched-out suspenders. His plaid flannel shirt is torn and reeks of gasoline. His thin, wiry black hair pokes out from under the manure-caked John Deere baseball cap on his small head. He's clanging a wrench against the cold steel innards of his tractor and sandblasting the air with an endless spray of profanity.

The vividness of this writing is achieved, in part, by the selection of verbs: *seeks, insisted, accumulates, obsesses, pours, corrodes, reeks, pokes, clanging, sandblasting.* Verbs are a writer's most potent medium. To learn more about using verbs effectively, turn to chapter twenty-nine.

Identify disturbances to your peace. Feel free to write about negative feelings. They are likely not to be reasonable, and rightly so. Feelings are different from reasons, but they are inarguably real.

List people who have done the following to you:

- irritated
- frustrated
- neglected
- abused
- manipulated
- repressed

Write to one of the following prompts:
- I seethed with turmoil when . . .
- "I can't take this any more!" I thought when . . .
- My neck and shoulders tense every time . . .

Read your rough draft aloud to someone who is supportive and caring, or listen the way an understanding friend would listen as you read this draft aloud to yourself.

⸏

Dave Chavez wrote about how his inner peace was poisoned and also about his response, his determination to "banish the inner demons of doubt, fear, and judgment" within himself. Twenty-five years after recovering from drug abuse, Dave found out he had hepatitis C. He says, "I've often let this legacy of doing intravenous drugs trigger fear and despair. Yet this and other painful events have also been catalysts that prompted me to search for meaning and see life's preciousness. It also became evident to me that God's grace, those unexpected and unmerited freebies, which help us through difficult times, spare us and teach us, takes many forms."

I made acquaintance with a woman this summer, who wrote me a parting letter, detailing the many faults she saw in me. It was very harsh and judgmental. Among other things, she told me that I was dying from hepatitis C. I found this incredibly insensitive and mean-spirited. She had no specific clues as to my diagnosis. The disease is fatal to a minority that have it. Mentally, I rebelled and challenged her assertion, all the while totally aware that I had foreseen visions of death on hundreds of occasions since being diagnosed.

I then realized how readily I distanced myself from negative doom-sayers, but how hard it was to silence my inner critic and nightmare visions. I would have yelled and cursed the presence of anyone who spoke so darkly to me about myself. Truly, I am my own worst enemy. How I wish I could become the inner friend I've always needed.

Sometimes when I think of how far I am from where I'd like to be, in terms of my inner qualities and behavior, I cry out, "Dear God, help me banish the inner demons of doubt, fear, and judgment. Teach me gently, to be gentle, positive, and thankful, for I feel there is a great desert in my soul."

To gather ideas for your second writing, first identify your sources of peace. Peaceful feelings are often associated with our senses. List sensations that soothe your spirit. The touch of a familiar blanket relaxes small children. You may be refreshed by the feel of summer rain on your skin.

- Touch that you find soothing
  - of a person
  - of an animal
  - of natural objects
  - furnishings
  - of tools or musical instruments
  - of clothing
  - of weather
- Sounds that soothe you
  - natural
  - musical
  - vocal
  - mechanical
- Sights that soothe you
  - outdoors
  - at home
  - in public places
- Smells that soothe you
  - from childhood
  - from the present
- Tastes that soothe you
  - beverages and foods associated with nurturing experiences
- Particular, calming thoughts
  - memories
  - passages from literature
  - poems
  - prayers

> **If you are writing with companions, share your list with a partner. You're certain to gain ideas from your partner's list.**

Some of us invite inner peace through the practice of personal rituals. We usually go to a quiet place apart from work activities and move into a space of time outside of tight schedules and pressing deadlines. The physical body is stilled first. Breathing deepens and slows. Gradually the mind becomes quiet.

When we pray, we are likely to focus on things in their individuality. When we meditate we may try to release all thoughts so that strengths and calm present in ourselves can emerge—and so that strength and calm beyond ourselves can be felt.

Be still and know that I am God.
PSALM 46:10
THE BIBLE

Many people find peace through certain activities. At the end of a cross-country ski trek, an acquaintance commented, "I didn't realize until we got back to the car that all the way into the lake and back, I was praying." His body was tired, but his mind was at peace. Prayer may be unfocused, as well as focused.

Ordinary chores can provide moments of peace: slipping one's hands into sudsy, warm water to wash dishes; weeding a garden; polishing a car; delivering meals to elderly people; rocking or reading to a child.

Noncompetitive communal activities frequently bring a sense of peace through harmony. They range from singing in a choir or crewing on a river to cooking in a soup kitchen, constructing housing for homeless people, assisting with disaster relief, and joining volunteers who pick up litter. Peace sometimes springs from humble, mundane sources.

List all the rituals and activities through which you find peace.

> **Exchange lists with a partner. Notice how your lists are similar and different.**

Write about a time or times when you have experienced inner peace. You may prefer to write about a particular occasion when you were filled with great calm, or you could write about the sources of peace that reoccur in your life.

～

Dana Furgerson teaches special education classes for students who have physical, intellectual, or emotional disabilities. At the end of her teaching day, Dana changes into her running clothes and lets her body outrace her mind. In the evenings she writes, and, as you will see here, she also gardens.

Gardening saves me from myself. Throughout my life, my gardens have given me refuge and tranquillity. I tend my garden and fall into myself and my imaginings. I find my soul's roots in my garden.

The smell of damp earth, chicken manure, and decayed flowers' stems and bean vines opens windows to my ancestral heritage of farmers in Ireland and Rumania. In my mind's eye, I see them stooped over rows of cabbages and turnips. They gauge how many hours of field work they have left in the day and what they must finish by dark. My garden becomes my survival, as gardens have always been for my ancestors. I tend, gather, and harvest in anticipation of the coming winter.

My soul opens to the Earth. My anxieties drain from me. What I should have done or shouldn't have done are of no import here in the garden. All that matters is balance. I am the gardener. I provide the care and nourishment to help my plants flourish.

I sing as my hands grasp, weed, and yank. I study the progress of vegetables as I murmur childhood rhymes. My fingers, hands and arms are smeared in dirt, streaked with pungent dandelion, and pricked and bleeding. At such times, if asked, I would say yes, leave me stay in my garden forever.

Lost memories come to me and linger. I treasure them, analyze them, grieve them, and giggle over them. Grandma Lupei, in her garden, works by my shoulder. The overgrown crooks and crannies of my garden become those of hers and my child self wanders there on sunny, summer days. Raspberries, strawberries, blueberries, grapes—the sweetness fills

*my head, and I am again the child gorging herself on berries, warm,
full, happy.*

*Whole days go by as I work and my mind wanders to my child-
hood, my marriages, my son, and my job. All assume serenity when
I'm in my garden. Life follows a rhythm in the garden. Rebirth
follows loss. Care and devotion yield harvest. Sun heats my back and
rain drizzles it. I balance my life in the garden.*

⟿

Find a peaceful time and a place where you can read aloud your
rough draft. Gently and appreciatively listen to yourself. Take note of
the ways you have found peace, and consider ways you can cultivate
yet more inner calm.

> **As you hear the drafts of your fellow writers, listen to discover paths new
> to yourself that you too could follow.**

Mary Ann Klausner is a counselor in practice in Eugene, Oregon. She
writes in her memoirs about how she finds inner peace after listening to
the turmoil and troubles of clients.

*I spend hours each day listening to the sorrows, confusion, longings,
and life dreams of clients who sit in my presence exploring and ques-
tioning their next life steps. They search for purpose and meaning,
connection and creativity.*

*I listen from my soul and mind and body as they reflect on their life
experiences, childhood, adolescence, young and middle adulthood. I am
impressed with their sincerity, their courage to unearth the pebbles, to
describe the currents of their own life river. I witness the integration
and joy they often discover in their everyday lives, the bumps and bruises
along the way, the faith they show in including me on their journey.*

*Yet the silence I seek to do the same type of reckoning often eludes
me. Five children are now grown and gone. The home in nature, built
on stilts, has now turned into a tiny cottage condominium with great
windows, white freshly painted walls, a front deck holding pots of gerani-
ums and morning glories. The television has been sold, the stereo is*

turned off. The telephone is rarely answered as I seek my own internal voice, the voice so many others have attempted to change through the years. I hear the crickets chirping out my bedroom window and glance at the stars and moon as they sit in the night sky. My interior voice is "growing louder, more insistent" and I remain committed to listen and honor it. Fifty-seven years' worth of experience, observations, perceptions, and curiosity have contributed echoes of sound, bouncing off the inside wall of my spirit, requesting my time and attention.

Write paragraphs in response to the following suggestions and questions:

- List any frustrations you dealt with that later resulted in peace.
- Has the distress you experienced made you stronger? If so, how?
- Where did you find comfort? Consolation? Liberation?
- What qualities in yourself enabled you to endure or overcome the turmoil you endured?
- What people have shown you the way to inner peace?
- When have you felt in harmony with your surroundings?
- Describe any occasions when you had a sense of completeness.
- What philosophies or beliefs have guided you to peace?
- Tell about any time when you felt in union with God.

When you write your final drafts, you might like to add photographs, copies of prayers, clippings, souvenirs, articles, or any other memorabilia that illustrates your writing.

Support us, Lord, all the day long,
until the shadows lengthen, and the evening comes,
the busy world is hushed, the fever of life is over,
and our work done;
then Lord, in your mercy, give us safe lodging,
a holy rest and peace at the last.

    A NEW ZEALAND PRAYER BOOK

      BOOK OF THE ANGLICAN CHURCH IN AOTEAROA, NEW ZEALAND,

        POLYNESIA

CHAPTER TWENTY-TWO
Dreams and Visions

The dream is the small hidden door in the deepest and most intimate sanctum of the soul, which opens into that primeval cosmic night that was soul long before there was a conscious ego and will be soul far beyond what a conscious ego could ever reach.

CARL GUSTAV JUNG

SWISS PSYCHIATRIST

I f you are attentive to your dreams, you'll find this chapter a potent medium toward understanding and revealing the emotions that underlie your conscious life. Even though you may be able to recall and write about only fragments of your dreams, those remembered, elusive, incomplete segments can provide insights into your soul. However, if your acquaintance with your dreams is sparse, you'll probably prefer to skip this chapter.

Dreams and visions may come while we sleep or meditate or whenever we are relaxed and receptive. Powerful dreams and visions sometimes appear to us during illnesses and catastrophes, and people have reported experiencing especially vivid dreams while they were anesthetized.

From ancient times to the present, the importance of dreams has been recognized. Their symbolic language is credited with prophesying the future, revealing the present, and explaining the past. Behind our conscious minds we discover unrecognized fears, wild happiness, and revelations about relationships.

In revealing our dreams we expose an unguarded part of ourselves. Honor your own dreams and the dreams of other writers. Dreams that appear to be nonsense may symbolically represent our psychological state. Absurd-seeming dreams may have underlying meaning and significance. Listen gently to all dreams, as they may be profoundly insightful and come from emotions deep within the dreamer.

Use one of the following prompts to write about a dream you had while sleeping or a vision you had while conscious. Write quickly without concern for accuracy.

- An especially vivid dream I remember . . .
- A recurrent dream I've had . . .
- A dream that awakened me was . . .

Recognizing that dreams are often macabre, irreverent, absurd, or even obscene, be prepared to accept your dream without embarrassment. Read your dream aloud to yourself or to anyone you know who is interested in dreams and is accepting of the uncensored, subconscious mind.

> **If you are writing with fellow writers, find a partner and read your dream accounts to each other.**
>
> **Ask your listener not to judge you by your dream and to acknowledge that you are not responsible for what you dreamed.**
>
> **A listening variation:**
>
> **Listeners may respond by asking the writer what the dream might mean. Listeners should not presume to interpret the dream.**

Gather ideas for more writing. Make brief notes about dreams, visions, or recurrent daydreams you have had that:

- frightened you
- reflected a struggle with a destructive power
- surprised you
- were about something or someone you had forgotten
- were telepathic, communicating with the mind of someone else by extrasensory means
- were clairvoyant, allowing you to discern objects not present to your senses
- were prophetic or indicated foreknowledge
- were synchronistic (coinciding with another event without causal relationship to one another, sometimes an inner event, such as a dream corresponding with external reality)
- solved a problem
- occurred when you were delirious
- occurred when you were near death or felt near death

- took you outside of your body
- brought someone to you who had previously died or departed
- were interactions with a higher source: a superior part of yourself or an external response to your need for help or clarity
- used metaphors or symbols to illustrate your situation

We are sometimes approached through nonvisual senses. You may have heard a person who was not physically present speak to you, or you may have sensed an invisible hand on your shoulder. A woman whose husband died several years ago reports smelling fresh whiffs of his cigar from time to time in their home. If you have had a similar nonvisual experience, make notes about it at this time.

Relating half-forgotten dreams helps return them to consciousness. Find a comfortable setting where you can forget your surroundings and look inward. With half-closed eyes, describe everything you can remember, accepting that your telling may be incoherent and incredible.

Though your dream or vision may be incomplete and seem unintelligible, you are ready to write about it. Don't attempt to make sense of it; simply try to include as many details as possible. Include all your senses that were affected: sight, touch, hearing, smell, and taste.

Tell how the dream made you feel.

John Pierce, minister of Westminster Presbyterian Church in Eugene, Oregon, related the following dream experience in his memoirs. As a young man John had intended to become a physician, so his undergraduate major was biology. He says, "Being raised in a highly critical home and educated in the scientific method has made me skeptical of my own experience. Maybe that is not all bad. Discernment must take place. That experience of Uncle Earl was the beginning of the numinous dreams I began having in my life and over which I have no control."

Along toward morning I had a dream. (There are occasions when dreams in Old Testament Writ are termed "night visions.") I dreamed I saw Uncle Earl lying on his bed. As I observed him I saw a figure in radiant white enter the room and step to the foot of the bed. I could not see his face but knew it was Jesus, though I cannot say how I knew. This radiant One reached out his hand, took Earl's hand, and pulled him forth from his body. It seemed as if the "real" Uncle Earl emerged from what had been the Uncle Earl I knew.

I sat up wide-awake and startled. Taking a deep breath I lay back down thinking that it's "just a dream. Go back to sleep." I knew my uncle was dying and this must be the workings of my subconscious churning in my sleep. In no more than two minutes, while lying in bed trying to calm myself, the phone rang. Early morning light peeked through the east window. My Aunt Margaret called to say that Uncle Earl had just died and she thought we would want to know.

∼

Read aloud your account and marvel at the dexterity of your clever subconscious.

If you are writing with other writers, exchange rough drafts and listen while your account is read by someone else. This act of distancing may help you better understand your vision or dream. As you listen visualize your dream as you would a fantastic tale told to you. Watch for symbols and motifs. Look at your dream as something apart from yourself.

Listen to dreams of other writers with readiness to marvel at the mind of the visionary.

Elaine S. Rudolph wrote the following entry as part of her "spiritual healing journey" while undergoing chemotherapy for lung cancer. During a meditation, two spirit guides—"I call them my teachers or my helpers"—came to her in the form of large birds like snowy egrets. Their eyes were compassionate and loving.

I hadn't thought about my Healing Temple for years. It had seemed somehow . . . outdated. I'd constructed it in my mind thirty years ago. It was—is—beautiful.

I gaze fondly at my glistening, white marble temple, taking in every detail: its perfect roundness, the arched entryway at the top of five stairs, the two luminous pillars on either side of the entrance. I can't see it yet but a large, translucent dome is the heart of my healing temple. Through the dome's portal beams a column of intensely bright, white light. It illuminates my marble healing table. Well do I know this healing Light! It is Divine, unconditional Love.

I yearn to be in my temple again . . . and of course here I am, climbing the steps with my helpers. We pass between the entry pillars and walk across the white tiled floor to my healing table. Reverently I place my hand on its cool, polished surface, remembering the unlikely, wonderful way it conforms to my body. So many times have I lain here and received healing. I glance at my teachers.

"Not yet, Elaine." Their voices speak as one while their long beaks reach toward me. With curiosity and awe, I realize . . . yes, their beaks are painlessly penetrating my body to withdraw the tumor.

"Corruption cannot survive the Light," they say softly as they place a small, dark mass on the table. I watch in fascination as the white light changes the ugly lump, ever so slowly, into a tiny pile of dry, gray powder that wafts away in the Light.

"It's gone," I say in wonder, knowing with absolute certainty it is gone for good.

"Now is your time on the table," they say, turning to me.

I'm lying comfortably on my cool, marble table. A bird teacher is on each side. I feel anticipation and joy. They lean toward me and their long beaks gently touch my skin. They are reaching inside my body with their long tongues to remove all remaining cancer cells. They carefully probe every cubic millimeter of my body. I understand when their search is complete and slide off the table to watch. Two long, sleek beaks carefully place minute, black dots into the Light. They become airy and waft away.

My bird helpers' gentle eyes hold mine. "Your healing is complete, but you must continue to take good care of your body, Elaine. Your body has become weakened and needs time to rebuild. Remember, the body's clock runs slower than the spirit's clock." I nod. Yes, I need to be reminded of this. It will take longer for my cure to become apparent to others.

～

Once in a while a dream's meaning is readily apparent, but reflection on most dreams yields further understanding. Take time to consider the following prompts:

- What images do you find in your dream?
- How might you interpret the images symbolically?
- What kinds of kinship or connectedness do you see reflected?
- Some dream analysts think our dreams compensate for our conscious attitudes. Because the ego has a limited perspective, the dream compensates by saying, "What about this?" The dream adds to our understanding to give us a whole picture. Has any one of your dreams functioned in this way?
- If your dream or vision suggests a parable, a short story that illustrates a truth or teaching, interpret it.
- Can you construe a personal myth from your dream or vision? Can the components of your dream be seen as symbols for your life as a whole?
- Explain how your vision does or does not offer solace and reassurance.

Revise your rough drafts if you wish to add thoughts. Give them titles, and proofread them for mechanical correctness. Write final drafts on acid-free paper.

To scrutinize a powerful dream can be disturbing. If writing about your dream causes you to feel overwhelmed, consider talking with a counselor who has been trained in dream analysis.

Most dreams appear to be enacted on the stage of our soul to teach us something. If we understand the dream, we can often recognize some of the forces at work in our lives and decide which direction we should move in.

MORTON KELSEY

EPISCOPAL PRIEST, PROFESSOR, NOTRE DAME UNIVERSITY

CHAPTER TWENTY-THREE

Encountering the Numinous

To Mercy, Pity, Peace, and Love
All pray in their distress;
And to these virtues of delight
Return their thankfulness.

   WILLIAM BLAKE

   ENGLISH POET AND PAINTER

The numinous is that which we perceive to be holy or divine. Our accounts of contact with the numinous reveal the pure flame of our souls, for in the presence of that which is sacred to us, we shed pretense and ego and discover our essence.

Individuals perceive the numinous in different ways. There is no one correct definition of sacred experience because, by definition, holiness is beyond comprehension. In this chapter you'll write about an experience of profound meaning that goes beyond rational understanding.

The writer of the following account grew up on a farm in Europe just before World War II. She has studied and worked in both Europe and the U.S. At this time she says, "I have known, loved, lost remarkable regular people and, now retired, write to tell our stories and what I learned."

An outsized event, the most amazing thing, one of those rare times when one is a direct witness to the miracle of life. One moment there was my body, large and aware of work being done inside it, of movements completely separate of my volition. But nothing could prepare me for the next experience, of looking at a person who never existed before and yet without whom the universe from now on was inconceivable. I saw the power of the incarnation of the life force and felt blessed, humble, and grand for having been the conduit for this manifestation of the great mysteries.

Even more delicious, it was a real baby with a strong small body, a little girl whose face eerily resembled mine, black hair curling on her head which a nurse had shaped in "a little curl in the middle of her forehead." She felt compact, resilient in her fragility, content to be. Her eyes in those first few days were the color of oysters, before turning dark, but already she had the steady, curious gaze I still love so much. She ate well and complained when she was hungry. That got me in trouble for a while as I could not resist her cries, fed her too often and got us both on an insane two-hour nursing schedule which exhausted both of us, until I had the painful courage to let her cry so we could both fully rest between larger feedings.

I knew then that I would truly give my life for her if it was called for. I never had, never would be so amazed, enthralled, and grateful for the immense power of life.

‿

This time you'll first gather ideas in preparation for writing.

Some of the ways we encounter the numinous, that which is sacred, are through our experiences with people, performing certain rituals or arts, and perceptions in particular places.

Chronicle times when you felt close to the Divine:

- Take notes on people through whom you have sensed the numinous

    people who embodied extraordinary compassion

    someone of any age who elicited unexpected goodness in yourself

    mentors who guided you

    someone who appeared to you in an apparition or dream

- List places that feel holy

    out-of-doors places

    a place of worship

    an unlikely place where, to your surprise, you sensed the presence of God

- Cite practices that have brought you into contact with the numinous
    a particular prayer or time of prayer
    meditation
    religious sacraments
    creative work
    music
    sports, dance, or exercise
    art
    expressions of love in all forms and relationships
    poetry and literature
- List animals or objects that conveyed the numinous
    a pet or wild animal
    a tree or plant
    a relic or holy object or memento
    a symbol or light
- Identify events not rationally explained involving
    intuition for which no rational explanation is apparent
    a voice
    a moment of heightened awareness
    a time of radical amazement
    a burst of joy
    a dream
    mental or physical healing
    the presence of someone or some being from afar

From your chronicle choose the subject ripe with energy, the one that feels most important to you, or the one that draws you. Some writers have identified a theme, such as music, under which they tell about numerous particular experiences.

Explain what was going on in your life at the time of your experience. Give background. Dare to confide what you might not state in public. After you've finished writing, you can decide whether to voice what you have written or to leave it quietly on the page.

Several possible ways of beginning this draft are:

- When I was . . .

- Whenever I hear/see/smell/touch, I remember . . .
- The most extraordinary event occurred when . . .

⌒

Pat Vallerand calls herself a "recovering attorney." After seventeen years of practicing law, she found the courage to quit her practice and embark on a new journey, one that has involved self-discovery, learning to live peacefully with the chronic pain of fibromyalgia, and unearthing feelings buried long ago in order to succeed in a very competitive and adversarial profession. Four years after quitting, she now works part-time as a mediator and arbitrator.

Here is her account of a hike along the shores of Waldo Lake in Oregon's Cascade Mountains.

On this occasion we were walking on the west shore in a vast forest of majestic old-growth firs. Below the gently swaying branches, the feet of these stately giants were carpeted in the striking green of moss and ferns. As we walked along in quiet companionship, I had an experience that I had never had before—and haven't had since.

It was a partially cloudy day, although dry. Not too hot, not too cold. The clouds were high and filmy. Clearly not thunderheads. Yet there was a feeling of energy, of electric charge, in the air. It seemed to be coming from the trees. I had the strong sense that the trees were trying to reach out to me—to communicate something that was important for me to know.

I also felt the energy within myself—at least "energy" seems like the best way to describe it. I felt filled with power. Not the kind of power I had ever felt before—not like the power I have often felt in my work as a lawyer, taking over a courtroom to fight for my client's rights. A very different kind of power. This was a healing, loving power. I felt it rising up in me, as if it were being poured down through the crown of my head into my feet and filling my entire body. I felt lighter, happier, and brimming with intense love; both love flowing into me and love flowing out. I felt compelled to exclaim (through my thoughts), "I love you," to all the trees and plants sur-

rounding me. And I heard them respond—the trees and plants were telling me that they loved me as well.

I reached my hands out, palms up, and felt joy and love emanating into and out of them. There was so much intense energy that I was afraid that if I actually touched something, sparks would fly.

I quietly described what I was experiencing to Cheryl, and we walked on in silence, enveloped in this love and energy. I felt as if I were floating. Colors and smells were intensified. I don't know how long we went on like this. In some ways, it seemed so brief; in other ways, the time seemed endless. I think we walked about a mile in this aura.

Why? What was the message I was to receive from this experience?

I have thought about that day many times since. It seems that what I was meant to learn was how to really accept love, to know that I am truly lovable as I am, and to know that the universe is safe, kind, and compassionate. Having felt that love and compassion, I can know that all experiences in life are ultimately positive. And, even more importantly, I can pass on that message to others, by conveying that love to everyone and everything I come in contact with.

When we accept the universe's love and allow it to flow through us, we become connected with each other and everything around us. In this connection we become the One—the spirit of life; there are no differences, nothing to judge. When we become the One, we are able to truly see the "forest." We are able to see that ultimate good comes from every experience.

You may be eager to share what you have written with people you know, or you may prefer to keep it to yourself. Let your feelings and inclinations be your guide. If you wish to read your rough draft to listeners, give them this advice:

"Many of us seldom speak of our encounters with the numinous because they go beyond scientific ways of understanding contemporary life. We fear we would be ridiculed if we related our experiences, so we guard our noncognitive knowledge in our hearts.

"As you listen to my account, set aside all skepticism. You are privileged to hear what can be confided only to a true friend. Withhold your own interpretation or explanation."

. . . negative capability, that is, when a man is capable of being in uncertainties, mysteries, doubts, without any irritable reaching after fact and reason.

JOHN KEATS
ENGLISH POET

Geraldine H. Crawford was working as a substitute teacher in Detroit, Michigan, when her adult son, Doug, was shot to death. Geri transferred from teaching to specializing in librarian/media services, and at this time she continues to use media skills by arranging audiovisuals for a Learning in Retirement organization.

No! It couldn't be! His body was there, but Doug wasn't there. That effervescent spirit, that curious and adventuresome boy who was always on the go, that compassionate person who was always helping someone and cheering people up, that raconteur who could tell me of his comic adventures now that he was thirty. I almost physically recoiled from the quiet stillness of his body and left the hospital room where it was. I murmured, "He is not there."

A chaplain was waiting for me outside the door. I began talking and talking incessantly to him, but I don't remember a word of what I said.

I finally left and found my car. Although the school policeman had driven me to the hospital, I drove home alone, but I couldn't stand being at home alone so I got into the car to go somewhere. . . . I decided to go to Doug's home. He and his friend, Cliff, were both social workers for Wayne County. They had bought the house and had planned to fix it up and make some money on it with their own hard work. I knocked and was let in. Several of Doug's friends and his recent girlfriend were sitting glumly around the living room. Some were drinking soft drinks and others beer—and then I spied the blood on the wall and the door leading outside. I knew immediately that it was my son's blood. He had given it willingly for a baby of a friend

*who had needed it, but NOT THIS violent act! All I wanted to do
was leave as soon as possible.*

*I got to my car. That blood was Doug's. It had struck me with
almost physical force. I fled in my car down the street, and as I did
I looked up and there was Doug! He said, "I understand, Mom. I
understand!" To this day, I believe it was his spiritual self speaking
from his heart to me.*

Do not feel that you must be able to explain your encounter with
the numinous. The numinous is defined as ineffable, or beyond our
understanding. Mystery is inherent. We describe rather than explain
such realities.

Make notes as you reflect on the following suggestions. Your responses are likely to help you tell about your experience more fully.

- If you transcended your usual limitations, tell what happened.
- Were mercy, pity, peace, or love aspects of your experience?
- Describe your spiritual empowerment.
- If you experienced divine presence, describe your perception of
  it as best you can.
- Numinous experiences are often said to be outside of time. What
  was the time frame of your experience?
- If you reached beyond yourself to unite with others, describe how
  you felt in the dimension you entered.

At this time you've probably written only one rough draft, but you
accumulated ideas for other drafts by listing times when you felt close
to the Divine. Write additional drafts from ideas you chronicled, or
place that list in your file.

You have revealed much of your individuality, your deepest feelings,
your soul.

CHAPTER TWENTY-FOUR

Spiritual Well-Being

Grandfather,
Look at our brokenness.

We know that in all creation
Only the human family
Has strayed from the Sacred Way.

We know that we are the ones
Who are divided
And we are the ones
Who must come back together
To walk in the Sacred Way.

Grandfather,
Sacred One,
Teach us love, compassion, and honor
That we may heal the earth
And heal each other.

    PRAYER OF THE OJIBWAY TRIBE
    A PEOPLE INDIGENOUS TO NORTH AMERICA

Our spiritual well-being does not necessarily correspond with our physical, economic, or social well-being. It's true that health of body and mind are linked and that physical health is affected by economic well-being. All the facets of ourselves are interrelated. However, spiritual well-being may or may not track with other ups and downs. Sometimes spiritual growth quickens when we struggle on other fronts.

～

As you gather ideas in this chapter, you'll chart different aspects of your well-being from your childhood to your present age. But first, warm up to writing.

Choose one of the following prompts, or create your own:

- A time when I had a sense of well-being in spite of difficult circumstances was when . . .
- My spirit was low when . . .
- My spiritual life intensified when . . .

⁓

One writer, Cheryl Roffe, began her rough draft this way:

One of the worst times of my life gave me one of the greatest spiritual gifts I have ever received. I remember getting up early on a cold March morning to have my meditation time before work. It was a gray, dripping, gloomy world outside, which reflected precisely what was going on inside me. I was terribly afraid because everything seemed to be going wrong in my life, and I already felt that the world was a grim place, full of pain and crisis.

As I sat on the couch in the little den that I used for meditation each morning. . . .

From this beginning, Cheryl related an experience that ended with her being "suddenly flooded with light, warmth, and a sense of well-being." At a time when major things were going wrong in her life, she arrived at a state of "quiet, intense bliss." Cheryl was spiritually very well in spite of what was happening to her, but the opposite can and often does happen. Your story might show either parallels or divergences between certain circumstances in your life and your spiritual well-being.

If you've written about a time you're glad to remember, it may involve someone with whom you are still in contact. If so, telephone that person and read this draft to her or him. If you prefer to mail it, read it aloud to yourself first and then write and mail a copy.

If you're no longer in contact with companions from the time you described, read this draft aloud to a young person, someone who will glimpse a dimension of you that you've not previously shown.

If you are writing with colleagues, read your drafts to each other.

When you are ready to revise this draft, reenter the experience you described by using the technique in chapter four. By remembering and reconstructing the drama you felt, you'll be able to add a sense of presence and dimension to your final version.

Adversity reveals genius, prosperity conceals it.
> HORACE
> ROMAN POET, 65–8 B.C.

Gather ideas for your next draft by charting aspects of your life. Look at the graph on the next page, and then, to make your own, turn a large sheet of paper sideways. Halfway down the page draw a horizontal line across the paper from one edge to the other.

Near the bottom of the page draw another horizontal line. Under it, write numbers in increments of five up to about the age you are now.

If you have colored pencils or pens, choose five contrasting colors to draw five different-colored circles in a row near the top of the page. Give the circles the following labels: "physical," "economic," "social/ cultural," "vocational/professional," and "spiritual/emotional." You'll use the corresponding colors to chart different aspects of your life on the graph. The following directions will be helpful.

Physical Condition

Think of the horizontal line across the midstrip of the graph as indicating average. If your physical health was below average when you were fifteen years old, place your mark below average at age fifteen. Use the color you placed in the physical well-being circle to indicate your health. When you had excellent physical health, bring the line above average. Your line will dip when you suffered injuries or illnesses and rise when you were in peak condition. Traverse your line across the graph from your earliest memories or knowledge about your health to the age you are now.

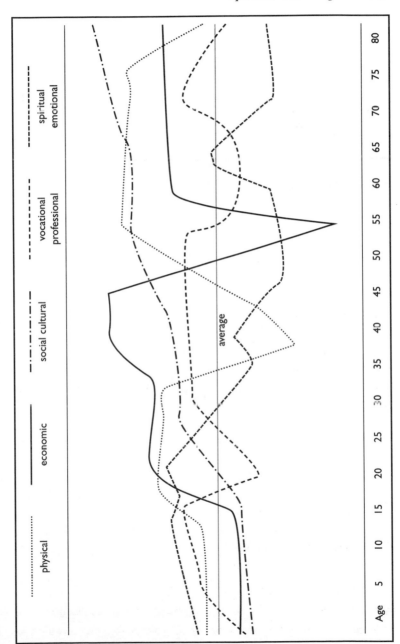

Economic Condition

After you chart your physical well-being, switch pencils or pens to use the color that indicates economic well-being. If your family was economically deprived when you were a child, place your indicator line below average; if your family was affluent, place your line high on the graph. Indicate your economic well-being throughout your life.

Economic well-being and the other categories are relative to personal expectations and experience. Your narrative, not the graph, is what will tell your story. If your family had few consumer goods but ate whole-some food, was adequately clothed and sheltered, and felt well-off, your written interpretation could explain any disparity between your place-ment on economic income charts and your sense of material well-being. For purposes of the perspective you'll gain from filling in this graph, mark your graph as objectively as possible, knowing the graph is only a device to prompt your writing.

Social/Cultural

Interpret the terms used on the graph according to whatever the words "social" and "cultural" mean to you. Define them for yourself. If you love going to baseball games and socializing at tailgate picnics and you have been privileged to enjoy many games and picnics, place your line high on the graph. Attainment of the educational and social goals you set belong here, too. This category also includes volunteer activities.

If you found yourself without friends or unable to take part in cul-tural activities, lower your line. Any way you mark your graph is proba-bly going to require written explanation. For example, if you were a student abroad living on a small stipend, you might have had few friends and been too poor to attend cultural events. However, the experience of living abroad would be rich in immersion in a new culture, so you would write about that complexity.

Vocational/Professional

When you chart this category, use the pencil or pen with which you colored the vocational/professional circle. Your childhood vocation was probably to be a student along with some added responsibilities. Your adult vocation might be the rearing of children and caring for members of your family.

Whether your analysis is subjective or objective doesn't matter as long as your writing tells how your work affects your well-being and how you feel about it. If, as a teenager, you had a job you considered good for someone under twenty, place your graph line high, but if you held a similar job at an older age when you wanted different employment, move the graph line down. Again, you will have the dilemma of deciding whether to place your mark according to external criteria or your own feelings. You could consider certain work excellent because you loved doing it, even though it didn't pay well; conversely, you may give a low ranking to lucrative work you disliked.

Spiritual/Emotional

Use your personal beliefs to define spiritual/emotional well-being. You could even decide to separate the two words and chart them separately.

Begin by writing a list on another sheet of paper on which you name the times in your life when you were powerfully attuned to such things as:

- intuition
- passion for knowing
- drive to do important work
- inspiration
- insight
- imagery
- meditation
- silence
- inner vivacity
- archetypes, or typical images and associations, motifs
- values
- motivation
- body wisdom
- imagination
- wonder
- compassion

Include any times when you felt:
- in communion with strength greater than yourself
- lifted beyond yourself
- filled with benevolence for all living things

Some writers evaluate their spiritual well-being from within the perspective of a particular religion, while other writers follow their individual sense of the meaning of the word "spiritual." Chart this subject in a way that corresponds with your own thoughts and feelings.

> . . . there's a spirituality that's a part of dance that I think I've been able to create. I don't go to church, but I have beliefs and I think that comes across in my dancing. I believe in God. It sounds sort of corny, but a lot of my inspiration comes from my spirituality. Sometimes it does feel like there is something that takes over my body. I'm not a different person when I dance, but I definitely go to a different level of existing.
>
> YVONNE BORREE, BALLERINA
> NEW YORK CITY BALLET

A good way to consider your spiritual well-being in relation to other aspects of your life is to see where the spiritual/emotional graph line deviates from or parallels with other lines. Ask yourself what the graph indicates. Some individuals have said their spiritual lives intensified and strengthened during difficulties, even calamities; other people have become dispirited at such times. Disappointment and grief can sap one's spirit. A chemical imbalance in one's body can rob spiritual vibrancy. Look at what else was happening in your life physically, culturally, economically, and vocationally when your spirit dipped and when it rose.

Carpenters use an instrument called a "spirit level" to ensure that the framework of their construction is plumb.

> spirit level—An instrument for adjusting any deviation from the horizontal or perpendicular by reference to the position of a bubble of air in a tube of alcohol or other liquid
>
> BRITANNICA WORLD LANGUAGE DICTIONARY

Your writing probably won't mention your graph at all. If you gained insights from the chart, then it has served its purpose. You can write about your spiritual well-being by telling about a certain significant stage in your life or by explaining how your spiritual life has changed over time.

Begin this draft any way you wish. Here are possible prompts:

- As I look back at different periods of my life, I see that . . .
- A time when I was spiritually strong though other aspects of my life . . .
- Over the years my spiritual life has . . .
- A way I now cultivate my spiritual life is . . .

⌣

Writer and poet Gail Winter says her "most profound healing has come from the written word." She is currently working on a book of poetry and prose chronicling her recovery from cancer, and she also facilitates groups of people who write journals focused on health and well-being.

We raised the kids with a little bit of both religions. Hanukkah candles and Santa Claus. Dreidels and Christmas trees. It was superficial spirituality. Religion without soul. And I knew it and pretended not to care. I was so conflicted about my own beliefs that it was truly the best I could offer my children.

All that changed dramatically with the first cancer diagnosis almost eight years ago. I remember coming home wanting to pray, but not remembering how. The prayers I had learned as a child felt woefully inadequate. I also felt hypocritical. So I sat cross-legged and repeated affirmations and visualized the cancer being eaten alive by Pac Man–type creatures. I eventually started meditating but didn't have a clue as to how to listen. So instead, I started visiting psychics. I was sure they could give me the answers I so desperately craved. I didn't know it then, but I see now that I was looking for the God I had turned my back on in my youth.

But there were no easy answers. I continued to grapple with my inner divinity, testing God, wanting proof of her existence. It has been a process of surrendering again and again to the mystery. I continue to question, as the cancer has returned a second and third time, why I am still alive and well. Have I won some sort of macabre jackpot? Is the gold in my body? A gold I was blind to? I hear the tinkle of coins and I know what? Nothing. I still have more questions than answers.

But there is a serenity today, a peace I have never felt before. It is a peace fought for on the battleground of my body. It fills my body and spills out onto the landscape of my life. It is what I now refer to as God.

⁓

To hear your rough draft, find a place of repose where, as you read, you can listen to the quiet wisdom from within yourself.

Some people have a friend whom they think of as a spiritual advisor. If you have such a friend, read this draft to that person.

Share your insights with your fellow writers.

Resolve to reserve time to do what nourishes your spiritual well-being.

Write brief, reflective paragraphs in response to the following questions:

- When has the spiritual dimension in your life been most strong?
- What people and beliefs have guided your spirituality?
- What people and experiences have enlivened your sense of selfhood?
- How has your spirituality changed during your lifetime?

⁓

Hy Schneider is a poet and short-story writer. He applied his talents to a long career in public relations that included planning political campaigns, as well as writing advertising copy. When he retired, he moved from New York to Oregon to live near his son and daughter.

I have been challenged to "write something spiritual," and, being a nonbeliever, I couldn't begin to attempt an intelligent and meaningful reply. Despite my many adventures, I was uncertain about how to search for an answer. There was nothing particularly spiritual about my experience as a soldier. I had five years of army life and found no spiritual clue. I was on a ship that was torpedoed and had been forewarned to "lay flat on the deck or you would be as flat as a country pancake." That was clearly not spiritual. I had a case of ammunition shifted from a huge truck to my inadequate shoulders, and its weight drove me into the wet ground like a tent peg, with no idea of my having had a spiritual experience of any kind.

However, the answer to my question was within me. My five-year-old daughter, who was then and will always be the apple of my eye, invited me to attend a party at her nursery school. We were playing a public game in which my daughter asked a question of me privately, and I would have to reply for all to hear. Her question was, "Do you love me?" and Victoria reached up and put her little hands on my pink cheeks and turned my eyes to her eyes and stared deeply and earnestly into my eyes as she whispered, "Everybody knows!" That's the closest I've come to feeling "spiritual."

PART THREE

The Rewards

CHAPTER TWENTY-FIVE

A Retrospective Look and Insights

To live content with small means; to seek elegance rather than luxury, and refinement rather than fashion; to be worthy, not respectable, and wealthy, not rich; to study hard, think quietly, talk gently, act frankly; to listen to stars and birds, to babes and sages, with open heart; to bear all cheerfully, do all bravely, await occasions, hurry never. In a word, to let the spiritual, unbidden and unconscious, grow up through the common. This is to be my symphony.

WILLIAM HENRY CHANNING
AMERICAN TRANSCENDENTALIST

You have traveled from the outer regions of your life, the territories readily visible to your friends and family, to an inner place where you have written about your greatest joys, intense longings, griefs, good intentions, hopes, and prayers. From this place deep within the labyrinth of your being, you'll look out upon your life with insightful perspective.

Before you do further writing, arrange for a quiet time when you reread everything you've written. Bring out all your chapters and parts of chapters, including the seeds of chapters stored in your greenhouse file. As you read, don't edit or proofread, but in an easy, pleasant, comfortable way, savor the fullness of all your writings.

The overview of your chapters will be revealing. You may see patterns in your life and characteristics in yourself of which you had not been aware. Look at the love you have felt and the ways you have expressed it. Notice where you have placed your resources, time, talent, and money. You will observe strivings and strengths in yourself to be appreciated. Take time to muse about your life and the subject of your memoirs, yourself.

As you write this retrospective chapter, you'll survey your life, and reveal some of your philosophy and values. Your contemplations may serve as a way of giving closure to your writings. They bring your voyage to its end.

⁓

To prepare for this writing, imagine that you have been alone in a tiny space capsule so long that you've lost track of time. You hear nothing, your capsule is controlled by remote means, and your food is a flavorless pabulum. You are with only your thoughts and memories.

If you find the idea of space travel appealing, then imagine a less literal way of being banished. Imagine that you are in isolation in a hospital bed where you are fed through a tube and forbidden to have television, books, or visitors. Day after day passes as you lie waiting to recover.

In your imagined estrangement, what parts of your present life would you miss? Imagine that from your space capsule or hospital bed you long to return home. Make long lists of the many pleasures you now enjoy that you would miss. Like the child at summer camp who whined that she missed the smell of her father's shaving lotion, when it was really her father she missed, include associated sensations, as well as the primary things.

List the things you will miss: seeing, touching, hearing, smelling, tasting, and kinesthetic sensations. (See the example on the next page.)

When your list is comprehensive, write to the following prompt:

- When I no longer live on earth, I shall miss . . .

Of course, you may rephrase this prompt.

⁓

Holly Reinhard wrote the following poem when she was only fifteen years old. As you can see, free verse is an option you might choose. Holly is schooled at home, but she takes advantage of writing workshops in Eugene, Oregon, where she lives with her family and dog, Caleb.

> *When I no longer live on earth*
> *I shall miss*
> *my mom,*
> *Talks we had, her cooking,*
> *The best spaghetti,*

Touch
Stan's beard
hugs from Claudia
Barney's fur
grass under bare feet
warm sand at beach
Minnie Gay's quilt
warm baths
silk Kimono
winter sun
wind lifting my hair

Sounds
wind in poplar trees
rain on roof
organ fugues
Mahalia Jackson's Ave Maria
tick of wall clock
drone of pump at the farm
music of Good Humor van
squeak of park swings

Sights
sunrise from the back porch
lilac bush in bloom
baby clothes on clothesline
fire in fireplace
icicles on eaves in sunset
Andy's face!

Unlike any other spaghetti, with meat and lots of chili
powder—though not too much.
I shall miss sticking my hand in the
flour when I bake something,
pushing a measuring spoon into the soft powder and making
molds.
I shall miss Caleb's mournful
bays and howls at sirens,
his coarse, black fur
silky
from the sun.
I shall miss running outside
in bare feet,
to greet my dad
when he comes home
from work.

Relish your draft as you read it aloud. If you are reading with friends, you'll feast on a banquet of pleasures.

～

One workshop participant wrote such a poignant catalog of tender moments she will miss that her group advised her to save what she had written to be read after her death at her memorial service. Many people do prepare suggestions regarding music they would like to have played and favorite verses they would like read at their memorial services. The writer's list showed the people and experiences most meaningful to her and will picture much about who she was if it is read when she eventually dies.

Laura Lyford, like Holly Reinhard, also used poetic form. Here are the first line and first stanza of her six-stanza poem.

When I no longer live on this earth, I think that I shall miss:

The alleluia sky of a glorious May morning,
The host of a moon over the Pacific on a warm August night,

The praying arms of oak trees silhouetted against a rainbow
sunset,
The grace of bird flocks practicing synchronicity,
The ever changing colors of nature as day calls out to day
And night to night makes every day unique.

Louise Yawger Cowan began her freshman year at Wellesley College in 1932 where she became number two on the varsity crew. She found that rowing as a team with seven other women gave her a sense of strength and power, and she loved the early morning call-outs when "the air was always fresh and cool, the campus peacefully burgeoning with spring and the lake unmarred by a single breeze so that the cox's commands rang out crisp and clear over the water."

Here she writes about an event at twilight.

On Float Night there were races between the class crews. Chinese lanterns hung at the bow and stern of each shell, glowing as darkness swept over the lake. At the end of the race all four crews came together to form a giant "W" and sing the alma mater. People watching from the bank sang along, and their voices echoed over the lake to us, resting on our oars in the gathering darkness.

Many years later, after she was widowed, Louise left her home on the East Coast and moved to Oregon, away from the friends and place she held dear. She told what she missed when she no longer lived in her home.

. . . I brought with me from New Jersey memories of days and nights in the little house on Division Avenue, of cold mornings by the fireplace in the kitchen, memories of waking surrounded by the lovely flowered wallpaper in my bedroom, the noises of shaving and song coming from the bathroom and the snuffling of the little black dog crawling out from under my bed looking for his morning walk.

Louise's memoirs show experiences she valued from the time when, as a young woman, she skimmed across the fresh lake in the early mornings to her later years when domestic routines had become most comforting and meaningful.

⸺

For your second writing, experiment with many of the following prompts to initiate a series of ruminations:
- In reviewing my life, my biggest surprise is . . .
- Something I would do differently if I could relive my . . .
- A satisfaction I have . . .
- A regret I have . . .
- My greatest joy has been . . .
- If necessary, I would have been willing to die for . . .
- A time when I felt awe/wonder/reverence was when . . .
- I hope that my grandchildren . . .
- My overriding concern is . . .
- My hopes for (name specific people you love) are . . .
- If I am reincarnated, in my next life I'll . . .
- I have faith that . . .

Reflect on your writings. Because writing stimulates thinking and discovery, actively take notes in response to the following questions:
- With whom or what have I felt union?
- What have I valued in myself?
- What have I valued in other people?
- Have I had a sense of mission?
- What has been my source of illumination?
- When have I felt compassion? Completeness?

Integrate your reflections into your earlier paragraphs or use them as additional musings as you bring your memoirs to a close.

What a wonderful life I've had! I only wish I'd realized it sooner.
COLETTE
FRENCH NOVELIST AND AUTOBIOGRAPHER

The following reflection is by Timothy Whitsel, a poet who writes and gardens near Springfield, Oregon, where he lives with his wife, Carol, and three children. For the past four seasons he has directed a monthly program of readings by local writers, The Windfall Reading Series, held in the Eugene Public Library.

Notice how Timothy's story moves from the description of a rollicking family meal to his reflections in the last paragraph about how we are measured and about grace. This memory and meditation exemplify a splendid final entry.

FALLING GRACE

There is no implant that will raise a dumb heart to care, to love, to delve. Time and again we must allow ourselves to be drawn in. Attention is no gizmo. Unless we can be lifted, we are old at any age. I know the light kindles in my eyes because I look at you. I do not stop. Set the table. We can eat and have our talk.

My father stood by the table one August evening. I must have been ten or eleven. Days and nights had been muggy, six weeks, without rest. Three boys with lightening bugs and boobs and baseball disappointments on our minds, we would not quiet down for prayer. Mom was frayed. And business anxieties had agitated Dad all summer.

Serving dishes were piled with food: sliced tomatoes and fresh-cooked snap beans from the garden, corn, pan-braised pieces of round steak. Dad raised his hand for silence. Then sat. As we began to bow, the wooden folding chair, by then advanced in use, creaked like a rusty gate unlocking, and collapsed. Before our half-closed eyes, Dad disappeared. Wrinkles of disbelief exploded on his forehead as he fell.

He never got to pray. Popping up like a dry cork, Dad danced a hootenanny jig to our volcanic laughs. The fartlek howls and giggles did not subside until the food was greasy chilled and night was thick against the window screens. We could not get enough. This is one of my staying memories of home and family and what works, by working not at all. The blessing that came by accident that night may happen any time we fall from grace, to grace.

Eternity begins in what we plant and how we tend; in time we all should be so lucky to be overgrown and, my gut says, we are measured (in the duff) not so much by what or how we change, but rather what we mend. Oh for luck to bless my children so, mending them by my falls and by the alacrity with which I rise to dance. Girls laughing, laughing decades later, laughing when a room seems empty, laughing unstoppably with their dancing fool old man.

If you have been writing with fellow writers, by now you have become intimate associates, bonded in trust and support. Travelers who make geographical tours together often feel a loss of camaraderie when the trip is over; they share addresses and resolve to stay in touch with each other. You who have voyaged together into the realms of your interior lives are likely to feel far more nostalgia as your expedition ends than land and air travelers feel.

Schedule a celebration. Invite each participant to read a selected chapter at your next gathering and to bring food to share.

If you have assembled and bound your final drafts by the time you meet, bring your book to show to each other. Chapter twenty-six suggests ways to put it together.

CHAPTER TWENTY-SIX
Your Book

A good book is the precious life-blood of a master spirit, embalmed and
treasured up on purpose to a life beyond life.
JOHN MILTON
ENGLISH POET

For many explorers the adventure is the goal; after it is over, they
are content to reflect privately on what they learned. Not all jour-
neyers want to produce a book.

You may be satisfied to have explored your inner life by means of
writing and feel no inclination to leave a written record. However, if
you would like to assemble your chapters into a book, read the following
pages for suggestions.

If You Have Not Written Final Drafts

You may have written numerous rough drafts that you haven't yet taken
time to revise and write in final form. If this has happened, simply use
your rough drafts for the book. The task of revising and writing final
versions of many drafts is burdensome, a chore likely to be postponed
and never done. It's much better to have an assembled book of first
drafts.

Consider how we cherish the handwritten diaries of our ancestors.
They are unrevised rough drafts. Proceed to follow the directions on
the following pages. You have accomplished the important part, the
writing itself.

A few people who haven't written final drafts do rally a burst of
energy, work within a specified length of time, and in a great flurry
complete their final versions; however, of the people who intend to do
this, most place their rough drafts in drawers, never find the time, and
evermore feel guilty.

Here is a solution. If you prefer a typed final draft but can't dispatch it yourself, hire a student or a neighbor who types, or a clever grandchild who has learned computer keyboarding, or hire a professional typist to do this task for you.

Of course, if you are writing for broad publication or for an academic class, then you will want to thoroughly and carefully revise and proof-read all your writings. Refer to chapters twenty-nine and thirty and assiduously apply those skills to each entry you've written.

Another Consideration

As you read through everything you've written, you may become aware that you avoided a difficult but important subject. This is not unusual. We often write around the most uncomfortable subjects, never about them. If this has happened to you, take time to imagine writing the words you've avoided. Quite possibly they should remain outside of your memoirs. However, often we find that the most difficult topics are filled with energy, depth, and power; in writing about them we discover still more spiritual dimensions in ourselves.

One way of handling this quandary is to go ahead and write about the avoided subject, but then put that chapter away for a while. Let several weeks go by before you look at it again, and then reread it in the context of your other chapters. At that time you'll probably have a sense of whether it should be included. Even if you decide to exclude this piece, you're likely to find that the writing of it was beneficial. To write about traumatic experiences is usually cleansing and can even lead to feelings of reconciliation. On the other hand, this piece may turn out to be the most dynamic and important part of your book.

> The man who writes about himself and his own time is the only man who writes about all people and about all time.
> GEORGE BERNARD SHAW
> IRISH PLAYWRIGHT, CRITIC, NOVELIST

Ask yourself if you want readers of your memoirs to know something about yourself that you've not yet told. You've reread all your chapters and looked through your greenhouse file. Look at the heart you filled with important subjects and at your lists of topics. Consider whether you've neglected an aspect of yourself; if you realize this is so, take time now to write about it.

Writing to Accurately Re-Create Reality

Even the most vividly written memoirs cannot replicate an actual event; some falsity is inherent because the best chosen words cannot duplicate the actual flames of experience. The writer can only mirror those flames, and in the process certain distortions occur. However, although slight discrepancy is inevitable, the underlying truth of your inner life will be apparent.

> The last thing that we find in making a book is to know what we must put first.
>
> BLAISE PASCAL
> FRENCH RELIGIOUS THINKER, MATHEMATICIAN, PHYSICIST

Parts of Your Book

The Title Page
You'll find a basic title page on the next page. Copy it or design your own title page. Notice that the word *memoirs* is plural. The plural form refers to autobiographical writings, while the singular form, *memoir*, has a different meaning: a record, note, or memorandum. You have written memoirs.

The Introduction
Write a brief introduction. Tell about your present circumstances, your age, and your involvements and interests. Describe your decision to undertake this current project, the writing of your memoirs.

Add a Photograph
The page following your introduction is a good location for a photograph of yourself. Identify it with your full, legal name and also with

The Memoirs

of

_____

WRITTEN IN _____

any nicknames. Place a caption under the picture telling what was happening in your life when it was taken.

The Chapters

One way of deciding how to organize your chapters is to spread them out on a table so that you can see all the titles. Then lay them out with the edges overlapping like a large hand of cards. Arrange and rearrange them until their order feels right. They can be arranged chronologically, in the order in which you wrote them, or in the order in which you'd like them to be read. Trust your intuition.

Bret Lott's memoirs, *Fathers, Sons, and Brothers,* interweaves chapters about his own father and brothers with chapters about himself and his sons. When he was ready to arrange and sequence the chapters, Lott placed them on his living room floor and physically moved them about.

Number pages consecutively from beginning to end. Handwritten numbers are acceptable.

The Conclusion

Your retrospective chapter is likely to serve well as a conclusion. Writers occasionally like to add further thoughts or a favorite meditation or prayer.

The Date

Write the current date on the last page.

Production of Your Book

Call the copy shop you prefer to use to find out if it carries acid-free paper. If it does not, buy the necessary quantity of acid-free paper from a stationery or art supply shop and take it with you to the copy shop.

An employee at the shop can adjust the machinery to make sharp copies of the photographs and documents you've placed in your manuscript. Faded exposures can be reproduced with increased contrast, resulting in copies clearer than the originals.

Buy binders for the manuscripts. Stores that sell notebooks are good places to shop. Look at the kinds of bindings that open and will allow you to add any chapters you may write in the future. If you want to have your book professionally bound, look in the yellow pages of your telephone directory under "book binderies." Many printing shops also bind books. Another option is the inexpensive "comb" binding that can be opened, available at most copy shops.

Share and Celebrate Your Book

With trepidation, trust, and love, give this most personal gift to the people who are dear to you. Consider also placing copies in the libraries of organizations and religious institutions to which you belong. The sharing of your life will open dialogues with other people and bring about gratifying new understandings and relationships.

> A good book is the purest essence of a human soul.
> SPEECH IN SUPPORT OF THE LONDON LIBRARY, 1840
> F. HARRISON'S *CARLYLE AND THE LONDON LIBRARY*

The Great Expedition

You have written earnestly and candidly about your inner life. You've shown your thoughts and feelings through periods of both difficulty and happiness. You've written about many of your dreams and struggles and the people and places most meaningful to you—and you may continue to write further chapters.

Your book shows your quest to find the meaning in your life. You may marvel at its ultimate mystery, or—if your expedition has been graced—you may have glimpsed your cup of completeness, of communion. You have shown the routes you've traveled, the signs that guided you, the lamps that lit your way; and in rereading the story of your trek, you may realize yet new territories to explore.

The Greater Fulfillment

Though the book you have written is valuable as a gift to its readers, many writers have found that the experience of writing is even more fulfilling than the satisfaction of having produced a book. The writing in itself may have been a spiritual experience. Yale Professor Jaroslav Pelikan said about the writing of *The Consolation of Philosophy* by the medieval philosopher Boethius:

"The very act of writing, the kind of dredging up of these questions and these tentative answers out of the past and out of the inner self— that very process, putting it down, trying to say it right, is the consolation. And so it is in the work of writing the work that the consolation comes, as it is in the quest that the finding comes. For a spiritual quest means precisely that: not starting in a vacuum at square one, but starting where we are with what we have and with what we have found, to quest for it again. In Augustine's beautiful term, it is *fides quaerens intellectum*—faith in search of understanding—so that, having found understanding, faith can search yet again. Over and over."

~

This final excerpt, written by a workshop participant, is longer than previous selections, but it is included because it is exceptionally insightful, beautiful, and is testimony to the power of introspective writing. Because the writer must remain anonymous to protect the confidentiality of her patients, she cannot be credited. Please remember her story after you have completed this book, and be inspired by it to continue writing the memoirs of your soul.

After my daughter died, I could not think of what to do with myself. Nothing made sense, the past had been swallowed by darkness, I could not even remember anything about her except for the last few weeks when life slowly seeped out of her. I could not project into the future, could not illuminate any part of the horrid eternal absence of her to guide my next step. So I instinctively continued what I had been doing, put one step in front of another, went to work every morning, fixed dinner every night, blindly, woodenly.

Reality did not cooperate with my wish not to feel, not to notice. I am a psychiatrist and my patients brought emotions which were dynamite. They spoke of being depressed, of wanting to die, wishing to kill themselves. Some knew that my daughter had died of suicide after many years of depression and remissions. But what could they talk about if not what was inside them?

And I was changing. I worried that I could not provide what my patients needed; I could not think as clearly as usual, my memory failed me. I had to look up the name and dosage of medicines I had used for years. I double-checked every decision I made, every prescription I wrote, terrified of mistakes. I consulted with colleagues to insure that my clinical decisions were based on the status of the patients, not on what had just happened in my family. Many of my patients were suicidal—it is the bread and butter of a psychiatrist's work—and I had always known that I stood firmly on the side of life for them. But now such stance was threatened by the immense love for my daughter, my empathy for her choice, my desire to join her. I knew that I could not offer the usual safe mooring to my patients.

In turn, their stories, their struggles, their pull toward blackness felt like cruel enticements to me in my fragility. I referred several patients to colleagues and tried to persuade others to work with a different doctor. But they would not, they cried that I was abandoning them, and I did not have the heart, the courage to oppose them. For weeks the situation weighted me down, I could not find peace, could not sleep.

Finally my body gave up and thereby rescued me in some fashion. Respiratory infection spread, resistive to treatment, and I finally had to give up when I could not speak anymore. A fitting end.

There were three months of the preoccupation of physical illness. I was weak, unsure, distracted by pain, in wait for others to find out what to do, which antibiotics would finally work. It felt right to be passive, not to be offered alternatives which my mind would not have been able to consider.

When I could think again, I came to recognize the dark coldness of depression. It was, I saw, very different from grief. Grief was a tribute to my daughter, a measure of her importance, of her stature in my heart which was gorged with love as well as sorrow. It was an alive feeling, as much as I hated being alive. It was an imaginative, *creative state, generous in giving me the sight of her face, the very texture of her skin on my fingertips, the weight of her body against my chest. I hated the absolute knowledge of her absence, and I loved the glowing knowledge of the life we had shared.*

In contrast, depression was subtractive, focused on my failings or errors in the self-centeredness of guilt and shame, and my heart became a bitter stone, small and immeasurably dense. It felt as if I were standing, with leaden feet, in the silently rushing waters of the river Styx. My consciousness was distracted and depression thus robbed me all over again of my daughter.

I fought it as I know how and it worked, little by little. Among other things, I decided to use classes; being a student has always been a pleasure for me. I had dreamt of retirement giving me time for art, and I enrolled in a class which brought back to me a welcomed awareness of color. The community college also offered adult creative writing classes. I thought I hated writing. I knew I was often late in completing paperwork, dreaded the dictation of long reports. Words were so weighty, the search so exacting to properly express and document findings, the consequences of incorrectness severe for patients and myself. But I have loved reading since childhood, have a great debt of gratitude to authors for the pleasure, guidance, and companionship they offered me. One class was titled "Women's Writing," a review of literature and creative writing combined, and that sold me on it.

The teacher had a lopsided charm, she was easygoing, enthusiastic about literature, lightly cynical about life. She chose lovely gems for us to read by U.S. and Canadian authors of the last 150 years. The group of students was generous in spirit, with an appetite for experience and the trust to share it, which lifted us above self-consciousness.

And the words came to me, unexpected gifts borne without struggle. They gave form to what I felt. For the first time I knew firsthand the alchemy of art, the passage from experience to expression which transforms pain into beauty, pleasure. What we wrote was not important stuff, yet profoundly meaningful. We played well together, appreciating spontaneity. I ranted, cried on paper and came out loving the whole thing. My classmates liked to hear my words, and I listened to, tasted theirs with admiration and gratitude. I wrote about now and way back when, sensing again the vivid course of life, no longer the frozen sludge of depression.

To stop practicing medicine had meant so many losses, of which I became aware in stages. Professional identity had been a big part of my self-concept for forty years. It had stood for goodness, dedication, intelligence, and I felt diminished without it. I missed the trusting exchange with patients, the warm connection with colleagues. I missed being a worker, rushing out of my office for a quick lunch downtown with all the other people who make things run. I replaced some of that by catching up on women friends, joining groups.

Only after I began to write though did I become aware of something precious I thought I had lost and missed intensely. As a psychotherapist, a unique part of my brain, psyche, spirit was engaged in a rich journey of discovery, using the patient's and my emotions as well as words. We communicated empathetically, intellectually, verbally, and it was my job to let the information collect inside me, feel it, taste it, weigh it, and to convey my sense of its meaning to the person across from me, using words familiar and cogent. After a few months of writing, as I sat with emotions, images, sensations, recollections, waiting for the words to come up that would describe them, I recognized that the same process was at work. I remember being washed over by a wave of gratitude, with surprise and joy. I was given back, in a new package, the gift of myself. With a casual toss of beneficence, life had even added new ways to manifest the gift of being.

The Community of Memoirists

Book in Partnerships,

s, or Academic Settings

Your literary expedition may be solitary, or you may enjoy writing with companions. Teamwork enables common people to obtain uncommon results.

This book is designed to be used by writers working together, as well as by individuals writing independently. Throughout the book, there are directions placed in boxes for people who are writing together. This chapter gives even more detailed suggestions for using this book with a writing partner, among workshop participants, and in college classes.

Using This Book With a Partner

A writing partner can be helpful in several ways. An ongoing, scheduled appointment with a partner will help sustain your writing momentum. If, before beginning to write, you talk to your partner about subjects you're considering, you'll automatically organize your ideas and find the right words. Once you've written a rough draft, your partner's responses will help you see its strengths and also recognize inadvertent omissions or ways it can be misconstrued. A good partnership energizes each writer and results in improved writing.

Use the guidelines throughout this book to respond to each other's drafts. These guidelines are designed to elicit constructive suggestions, protect your confidentiality, and shield you from personal criticism.

To find a writing partner:

- Let your friends and acquaintances know you're looking for a fellow writer.
- When you're among associates, announce that you're looking for a writing partner.
- If your community has a literary guild or community center where

The Community of Memoirists

CHAPTER TWENTY-SEVEN

Using This Book in Partnerships, Workshops, or Academic Settings

writing is taught, telephone to ask how critiquing groups are formed.

- Consider posting a "want ad" in a building where religious services are held.

Family members are not always ideal writing partners. Relatives tend to "correct" one's memories, to be judgmental, and to be less tactful than people from the outside. However, if a relative wants to write with you and is willing to follow the listening guidelines, you're likely to form a close familial bond in addition to writing your spiritual memoirs.

Couples who write together will see facets of their partners they might otherwise never glimpse. The resulting insights can lead to deeper understanding, increased appreciation, and greater spiritual intimacy.

To Use This Book in a Workshop

This book is readily usable by many kinds of groups: writers organizations, lifelong learners, members of religious congregations, support groups, renewal institutes, and people who seek to examine and understand their lives. To use this book as a workshop guide or text, you should follow the boxed instructions. Each chapter fits a two-hour session. To maintain group cohesion and momentum, plan to meet every week.

Participants in full-time, intensive summer workshops can meet daily and complete a chapter a day. All the chapters following chapter three initiate two writings. If participants meet mornings and afternoons, they will have time to take the warm-up writing through all the steps of the writing process during the morning and do the same with the second topic in the afternoon.

To organize a workshop, you'll first need to find a meeting location. In Eugene, Oregon, the Pastoral Care Department of a large hospital sponsored the class and arranged for two different workshops to meet in hospital conference rooms on Saturday mornings and Sunday afternoons. In some communities, public utility companies allow community groups to use their meeting rooms, and a few banks make their conference rooms available on Saturdays. Independent bookstores frequently agree to remain open on certain evenings for literary groups. You may be able to use a room belonging to a religious organization, senior center, lifelong learning school, local writers group, or even the place where you work. People who don't drive or don't own cars will appreciate a location near public transportation.

Attract people to your workshop by sending announcements to your local newspapers, literary organizations, and publications for retired people. You may also wish to include newsletters written for religious groups and the organizations to which you belong, as well as the in-house letter of the business providing your meeting place. Be aware that newsletter editors often need to receive stories about a month before delivery time. Enclose page-size posters for bulletin boards along with your newsletter announcements. You may also be able to staple posters on bulletin boards in recreation centers, bookstores, shops, libraries, and places of worship.

Enrollment should be limited to twenty people. If more people wish to enroll, make a waiting list or schedule an additional section. Participants usually prefer to commit themselves for only eight sessions at a time, with assurances that they may reenroll for continuing sessions.

Plan to hold special celebratory sessions after every eight chapters are completed, beginning with chapter three. On these occasions invite participants to read selections from their writing to the group at large. Ahead of time announce that readings will be limited to a certain number of minutes so that no one will monopolize the event, and continue to enforce the guidelines for good listening. Some members of the group may prefer to listen only, but the majority of participants will want to read. Such events are a highlight of the workshop.

Critical to a successful workshop is the creation of a safe atmosphere. The workshop facilitator must ensure that listeners refrain from judging the behavior, lifestyles, and feelings expressed by the writers, and that members of the workshop guard the confidence of every writer. Discuss the guidelines for good listening the first time you meet, and remind participants of them at the next several sessions.

Advice for Instructors, Facilitators, Teachers, and Professors

The instructor or workshop leader should always write rough drafts along with participants. To expect them to disclose their inner lives while withholding one's own personal life does not create a participatory atmosphere. A teacher may choose not to reveal herself as fully as she would if she were writing among her peers; nevertheless, she must participate in both the writing and responding in order to create comfort and enthusiasm in the students. The response groups provide an opportunity to build collegiality.

When the instructor or leader takes part in response groups, he should not assume the role of facilitator. Participants, even younger students, should be the ones to decide who will read first and when to move on to the next reader. By following the guidelines for listening and responding, students and participants are perfectly able to manage the response groups themselves, and they gain assuredness by doing so.

As your group works toward the following chapters, please alert participants so they will make certain preparations:

• Chapter eleven—bring a snapshot picturing a person, place, or object important to the writer.

• Chapter eighteen—bring a thing that is meaningful to the writer such as a prayer, poem, work of art, selection of music, handmade item, passage of literature, saved letter, or cherished gift.

• Chapter twenty-four—bring pencils or pens in at least five different colors to draw lines.

• Chapter twenty-five—reread everything written.

Since the writing of Saint Augustine's *Confessions,* the confession has been a component of memoirs. Whenever we reflect on our inner lives, we confront the acts we have suffered and the deeds we have committed. Confession is inevitable. You must create a safe environment so participants can explore their deepest troubles as well as their great joys. You must not be shocked by any revelations. Though you will be confronted with confidences you didn't expect, you must remain accepting and empathetic.

Sometimes writers will bring narratives for you alone to read. Those writers aren't ready to share what they have written with response groups, and their writing may reveal suffering that will distress you. When the next workshop or class meets, find a time when you can speak quietly and privately to the writer. Thank that person for placing trust in you and commend her for being able to write about the problem. Then, if it seems appropriate, ask the writer if she has found a good counselor. Most writers will say that they have, but if someone has not found a helpful counselor, be prepared to suggest resources. Have ready appropriate telephone numbers for mental health services, rape crisis counselors, or other suitable hot lines. Do not attempt to counsel the writer yourself unless you are a professionally trained, licensed, and insured counselor.

To write about what we have suffered, both as victims and inflictors, is cleansing and healing. Writing expels the experience from deep within oneself and allows one to examine it and somewhat dissociate from it. Through such writing we are sometimes able to forgive, to find forgiveness, and to regain self-respect. You are honored with trust when made part of this process.

To Use This Book as a Course Textbook

. . . we have an opportunity to revision education as a communal enterprise from the foundations up—in our images of reality, in our modes of knowing, in our ways of teaching and learning.

In such an education, intellect and spirit would be one, teachers and learners and subjects would be in vital community with one another, and a world in need of healing would be well served.

PARKER J. PALMER

EDUCATIONAL REFORMER AND WRITER

Memoirs of the Soul is ideally suited to grade-free classes, but it can also be used as a college credit class text if the instructor evaluates the students' work according to adherence to the steps of the writing process, participation in response groups, and mastery of writing skills rather than the content of students' memoirs. At each class students should hand in both their rough drafts, showing editing and proofreading marks, and their final drafts.

As the instructor reads final drafts, she can assess the students' needs for instruction in the conventions of standard English and then provide it. Usage and style should be taught as well as standard conventions. William Strunk Jr. and E.B. White's *Elements of Style* and William Zinsser's *On Writing Well* are excellent texts to use.

If the instructor follows the chapters in this book as they are sequenced, the students' writing will follow a classical literary form in which the first chapters delineate characters and place and reveal the main character's goals and problems. These chapters are followed by rising action and complications that lead to one or more crises. Dramatic tension mounts until it reaches a climax, the moment when we see what the outcome will be; after that, a resolution, or dénouement, reveals how the main character comes to terms with all that has happened. In a loose, general way, the chapters of this book will shape students' memoirs according to classical, literary form. (See the chart on the next page for more details.)

Look at the next chapter to find suggested lists of writers guides, memoirs and autobiographies, anthologies, and books of particular interest to instructors and workshop leaders. These lists can be changed or extended according to the instructor's purpose and preferences.

Ask students to write reviews of the published memoirs and autobiographies they read and also to make copies of their reviews for all members of the class. Everyone enrolled will thus accumulate collections of their peers' reviews, a helpful guide as they choose which books they want to read. Collections of reviews from past classes can comprise a small library for use by current students.

The instructor should consider also requiring students to keep dialogic journals of their readings. To keep a dialogic journal, the reader folds a page of lined paper vertically. To the left of the fold, the reader copies any phrase or sentence from the book that elicits his reaction, whether of agreement, disagreement, surprise, or any other emotion. To the right of the fold, the reader writes to the author or to one of the characters in the book. The reader may argue, advise, congratulate, or engage in any other form of dialogue. The vertically folded paper is

delineation of characters and circumstances —
- Subjects for Your Memoirs
- Breathing Life Into Your Writing
- Internalized Places
- The Soul of a Child
- People Who Etched an Imprint
- Adolescent Angst
- Events That Shaped the Course of Your Life

rising actions —
- Struggles and Satisfactions
- Focusing on Your Subject
- Transitions
- Joinings and Separations
- Chance and Choice
- Aspirations
- Evolving Ideas About Religion

climaxes and revelations —
- Confronting Crisis
- Longings
- Love
- Flip of the Compass
- Inner Peace
- Dreams and Visions
- Encountering the Numinous

dénouement —
- Spiritual Well-Being
- A Retrospective Look and Insights

used for a bookmark so the reader can conveniently add to it while reading the book. If the reader rages or philosophizes in response to the author, the journal can grow to numerous pages in length. The keeping of a dialogic journal engages the reader and is useful later when writing a book review. Grade the journal according to the amount of understanding and involvement with the book it shows, not by whether the reader agrees or disagrees with the perspective of the author.

Grades can be based on:

- completion of a designated percentage of writing assignments
- incorporation of the steps of the writing process
- unfailing participation in response groups
- conformity of final drafts to the conventions of standard English and the elements of style taught by the instructor
- thoughtful dialogic reading journals
- analytical book reviews

If you ask students to use these six criteria to grade themselves, they will reflect on their efforts as well as their achievements. Most students grade themselves more severely than we would grade them, and you will have the pleasure of raising some of their grades.

The basis for grades should be made clear in the course description and syllabus. It should also be stated that the instructor will not judge the content of the students' memoirs and will guard the confidentiality of every student's writing.

Several chapters in this book should be optional, if used at all, in courses for credit. They are chapters seventeen, nineteen, twenty-two, twenty-three, and twenty-four. Some of the workshop participants who have used this book found that they were not ready to confront the major crises in their lives. They said they might return to chapter seventeen later, when they feel emotionally ready to look at traumas they are not yet able to face. Chapters twenty-two and twenty-three open subjects students may feel strange disclosing in a credit course, and chapter nineteen could be uncomfortably revealing and personal for some students. Chapter twenty-four requires experience and perspective younger students may not yet have. All of these chapters are valuable for individuals who write their spiritual memoirs but may be inappropriate, and certainly should be optional, in graded classes.

Instructors of graded courses should require all students to take part in the response groups for all the assigned chapters, but allow students to indicate which final drafts they want to submit for grades. Not every topic will work equally well for every writer, and not every final draft has to be graded.

Using This Book at the Secondary Level

Some chapters of this book are not appropriate for use with secondary students because high school students tend to be less compassionate as peer editors than adults. Adolescents are not yet sure of their own identities, so they are more likely to discuss classmates' disclosures. Immature students are likely to tell their friends what they heard revealed.

However, if you do choose to use *Memoirs of the Soul* as a textbook, you might begin the course by first discussing the steps of the writing process and then the problem of confidentiality. You must obtain an agreement of confidentiality from the class. If the students themselves discuss the potential for harm from peer gossip and then design their own confidentiality code, they are more likely to observe it. Encourage them to create a formal pledge of confidentiality that every class member would sign.

Reassure students that you will not call their parents or talk about the students' writings in the teachers' lounge. However, another issue that could arise if this book is used at the secondary level is the requirement placed on teachers to report indications of child abuse or intention to do harm. When students write about personal aspects of their lives, revelations of this nature can occur. Explain to your students at the beginning of the course that you are required to inform counselors of abusive or dangerous situations. Because writing is a powerful tool for healing, most students do benefit from writing about painful parts of their lives, but they should be aware that a counselor might have to be alerted.

Memoirs of the Soul is a prescriptive book only in terms of method.

It should never be used for doctrinaire purposes. Because it invites disclosure, a well-meaning teacher could do great damage if she or he were to try to "correct" the feelings and thoughts of the writer. Teachers, as well as students, must follow the guidelines for listeners. A sensitive teacher might, at the time when listeners ask questions, pose a question that would guide the writer toward self-examination, but any judgmental response would violate the trust and the integrity of the writer.

Let us be united;
Let us speak in harmony;
Let our minds apprehend alike.
Common be our prayer;
Common be the end of our assembly;
Common be our resolution;
Common be our deliberations.
Alike be our feelings;
Unified be our hearts;
Common be our intentions;
Perfect be our unity.

FROM THE RIG VEDA
ANCIENT HINDU HYMNS OF PRAISE

CHAPTER TWENTY-EIGHT
Suggested Reading List

Writing Skills Books
Elements of Style, William Strunk Jr. and E.B. White
On Writing Well, William Zinsser
Writing With Power, Peter Elbow

Memoirists' Guides
Inventing the Truth: The Art and Craft of Memoir, William Zinsser, Editor
Going on Faith: Writing as a Spiritual Quest (formerly published as *Spiritual Quests*), William Zinsser, editor
Telling Your Story, Sam Keen
The Artist's Way: A Spiritual Path to Higher Creativity, Julia Cameron
The Story of Your Life: Writing a Spiritual Autobiography, Dan Wakefield
Writing as a Way of Healing, Louise DeSalvo
Writing the Natural Way, Gabriele Rico

Memoirs and Autobiographies
The books on this list represent a variety of perspectives and cultures. The list is deliberately eclectic, and the books are not annotated because part of the adventure involves rummaging in libraries, picking up unfamiliar books, skimming them, and deciding whether to venture into the lives they open or to return them to the shelves. If an enticing title is not housed in your library, ask the reference librarian to order it for you through interlibrary loan.

May you discover new realms of thought and feeling that will expand your understanding and the dimensions of your own spirituality.

A Leg to Stand On, Oliver Sacks
A Life in School: What the Teacher Learned, Jane Tompkins
A Long Way From Tipperary, John Dominic Crossan

A Portrait of the Artist as a Young Man, James Joyce

A Romantic Education, Patricia Hampl

A Sort of Life, Graham Greene

A Walker in the City, Alfred Kazin

A Woman of Egypt, Jehan Sadat

About This Life, Barry Lopez

All but My Life, Gerda Weissmann Klein

Alone Together, Elena Bonner

An American Childhood, Annie Dillard

An Unquiet Mind, Kay Redfield Jamison

And No Birds Sang, Farley Mowat

Apologia Pro Vita Sua, John Henry Newman

Autobiography of a Yogi, Paramhansa Yogananda

Autobiography: The Story of My Experiments With Truth, Mohandas Gandhi

Black Elk Speaks, John Neihardt and Nicholas Black Elk

Blessings in Disguise, Alec Guinness

Blowing Zen: Finding an Authentic Life, Ray Brooks

Breaking Barriers: A Memoir, Carl T. Rowan

Cave in the Snow: Tenzin Palmo's Quest for Enlightenment, Vicki Mackenzie

Cloister Walk, Kathleen Norris

Confessions, Jean-Jacques Rousseau

Confessions, Saint Augustine

Dakota: A Spiritual Geography, Kathleen Norris

Days of Obligation: An Argument With My Mexican Father, Richard Rodriguez

Death Be Not Proud, John Gunther

Diary of a Zen Nun, Nan Shin

Dust Tracks on a Road, Zora Neale Hurston

Fathering Words: The Making of an African American Writer, E. Ethelbert Miller

Fathers, Sons, and Brothers, Bret Lott

From My Life: Poetry and Truth, Johann Wolfgang von Goethe

Grey Is the Color of Hope, Irina Ratushinskaya

Growing Up, Russell Baker

Hope Against Hope: A Memoir, Nadezhda Mandelstam
I Know Why the Caged Bird Sings, Maya Angelou
In My Own Way: An Autobiography, Alan Watts
In Search of Sugihara, Hillel Levine
Journey Into the Whirlwind, Eugenia Semyonovna Ginzburg
Leaves From the Notebook of a Tamed Cynic, Reinhold Niebuhr
Life in a Day, Doris Grumbach
Life in a Jewish Family, Edith Stein
Living Faith, Jimmy Carter
Long Quiet Highway, Natalie Goldberg
Looking for Mary (or, the Blessed Mother and Me), Beverly Donofrio
Lost in Place: Growing Up Absurd in Suburbia, Mark Salzman
Meditations From a Movable Chair, Andre Dubus
Memories of a Catholic Girlhood, Mary McCarthy
Memoirs, Natalya Dolgorukaya
Memoirs, Raisa Orlova
Memoirs of a Dutiful Daughter, Simone de Beauvoir
Memoirs of Childhood and Youth, Albert Schweitzer
Memories, Dreams, Reflections, Carl Gustav Jung
Miriam's Kitchen, Elizabeth Ehrlich
Motherhouse, Jeanine Hathaway
Narrative of the Life of Frederick Douglass, An American Slave: Written by Himself, Frederick Douglass
New York Jew, Alfred Kazin
Not Even My Name, Thea Halo
Notes of a Native Son, James Baldwin
One Writer's Beginnings, Eudora Welty
Ordinary Resurrections: Children in the Years of Hope, Jonathan Kozol
Paula, Isabel Allende
Plant Dreaming Deep, May Sarton
Reason for Hope, Jane Goodall
Refuge: An Unnatural History of Family and Place, Terry Tempest Williams
Report to Greco, Nikos Kazantzakis
Returning: A Spiritual Journey, Dan Wakefield
Salvation on Sand Mountain, Dennis Covington

Seduction of the Spirit, Harvey Cox
Speak, Memory, Vladimir Nabokov
Surprised by Joy, C.S. Lewis
Telling Secrets, Frederick Buechner
The Autobiography of Eleanor Roosevelt, Eleanor Roosevelt
The Autobiography of Malcolm X, Alex Haley
The Barn at the End of the World: The Apprenticeship of a Quaker, Buddhist Shepherd, Mary Rose O'Reilley
The Close: A Young Woman's First Year at Seminary, Chloe Breyer
The Color of Water: A Black Man's Tribute to His White Mother, James McBride
The Consolation of Philosophy, Boethius
The Dance of the Dissident Daughter, Sue Monk Kidd
The Dark Child, Camara Laye
The Delights of Growing Old, Maurice Goudeket
The Diary of Helena Morley, translated and edited by Elizabeth Bishop
The Diving Bell and the Butterfly, Jean Dominique Bauby
The Imitation of Christ, Thomas à Kempis
The Magic Lantern, Ingmar Bergman
The Measure of a Man: A Spiritual Autobiography, Sidney Poitier
The Names, N. Scott Momaday
The Night Trilogy: Night, Dawn, the Accident, Elie Wiesel
The Pilgrim's Progress, John Bunyan
The Promised Land, Mary Antin
The Seven Storey Mountain, Thomas Merton
The Story I Tell Myself, Hazel E. Barnes
The Trembling of the Veil, William Butler Yeats
The Woman Warrior, Maxine Hong Kingston
The Words, Jean-Paul Sartre
Things Held Dear: Soul Stories for My Sons, Roy Herron
This House of Sky: Landscapes of a Western Mind, Ivan Doig
Through the Narrow Gate, Karen Armstrong
Traveling Mercies: Some Thoughts on Faith, Anne Lamott
Turbulent Souls: A Catholic Son's Return to His Jewish Family, Stephen J. Dubner

Up From Slavery, Booker T. Washington
Visions of Glory: A History and a Memory of Jehovah's Witnesses,
    Barbara G. Harrison
Walden; Cape Cod; The Maine Woods, Henry David Thoreau

Anthologies
God: Stories, C. Michael Curtis, editor
*Searching for Your Soul: Writers of Many Faiths Share Their Personal
    Stories of Spiritual Discovery*, Katherine Kurs, editor
The Best Spiritual Writing, Philip Zaleski, editor

Books of Particular Interest to Instructors and Workshop Leaders
*Guiding Autobiography Groups for Older Adults: Exploring the Fabric
    of Life*, James E. Birren and Donna E. Deutchman, The Johns
    Hopkins University Press
*The Meaning of Lives, Biography, Autobiography, and the Spiritual
    Quest*, Richard A. Hutch, Reader in Religion and Psychological
    Studies, University of Queensland, Wellington House, 125
    Strand, London, WC2R OBB, England; also P.O. Box 605,
    Herndon, VA 20172
The Spiritual Side of Writing, Releasing the Learner's Whole Potential,
    edited by Regina Paxton Foehr and Susan A. Schiller, Boynton/
    Cook Publishers, Heinemann
When Memory Speaks: Exploring the Art of Autobiography, Jill Ker
    Conway, Alfred A. Knopf/Rand
Writing and Healing: Toward an Informed Practice, edited by Charles
    M. Anderson and Marian M. MacCurdy, National Council of
    Teachers of English, Urbana, IL
*Writing Your Heritage: A Sequence of Thinking, Reading, and Writing
    Assignments*, Deborah Dixon, National Writing Project, Berkeley,
    University of California
*Your Life as Story: Discovering the "New Autobiography" and Writing
    Memoir as Literature*, Tristine Rainer, Tarcher/Putnam, New
    York

PART FIVE

The Skills

CHAPTER TWENTY-NINE

Suggestions for Revising Rough Drafts

To revise is to put in, take out, transform, and flip about.

Revision is optional for those people who are writing for themselves and a few close friends. The majority of writers do find that their quick rough drafts are much improved when revised, but some writers don't like to revise, and others are satisfied with rough drafts.

If your memoirs might be seen by people in your community and saved by your descendants, then you probably want to express yourself as effectively as possible. Look upon revision as an opportunity to strengthen and enrich your writing. Revision, unlike proofreading, can be marvelously creative.

If you are writing your memoirs for broad publication or as part of an academic course, then you will find revision essential for the production of high-quality work. In fact, you may want to ask your response group not only to point out strengths in your writing and pose questions but also to report their personal responses to your writing and make suggestions. Every time you meet, bring a copy of your rough draft for each member of your response group so that as you read aloud everyone can follow visually and write comments on your draft. Ask your listeners to return their annotated copies to you so you can carefully consider all their remarks before writing your revisions.

Most professional writers spend far more time revising than they spend writing first drafts. Paul Valery, an esteemed French writer renowned for his style, said that great writers never finish revising their work; eventually they must abandon it.

We don't revise as we write the original draft because to do so would interrupt the voyage. It would slow us down, causing us to lose sight of what's ahead. We would miss the upcoming turn; we might not even get to the upcoming turn. Instead of steering by the stars, we would be stumbling over rocks. Travel with the meteoric rush of words in your first draft, knowing you can edit them later.

The ideal time to revise your writing is after you've heard it read aloud and after you've answered the questions suggested for reflection.

Revision should be completed before you proofread for mechanical correctness, that is: spelling, punctuation, capitalization, paragraphing, grammar, and correct word usage. Postpone proofreading until just before you write the final draft.

Add to Your Rough Draft

Provide Necessary, Supplementary Information

You'll probably first want to add information. Your oral reading and listeners' questions have revealed what needs to be clarified. When we hear listeners' responses to readings, we often realize we've inadvertently left out essential information. A middle-aged writer recounted an incident that happened when she was sixteen, but she failed to mention that she had been a teenager at the time. When she saw the effect her story had on listeners, she realized at once that she needed to add information about her age. Note listeners' questions in your margins so that later, when you revise the account, you'll remember what further information may be needed.

If you do add information, make use of the alternating blank lines. You may also write supplementary paragraphs to insert in the appropriate places. Expand your draft as much as necessary to make the chapter complete.

Add Sensory Data

When you wrote your rough draft, you wrote rapidly and impulsively. You followed your story wherever it led. You made a quick sketch. Now you're ready to add sensory description.

Smell is the most evocative sense, but writers who don't know this frequently forget to include it. Realtors know the importance of smell. Some realtors arrive at a house before it is shown to bake cookie dough in the oven so that when prospective buyers walk in the door they'll feel that the house is homey and inviting.

Smell and taste can be more challenging to convey with words than the other senses; sometimes you'll need to make comparisons. For example, the smell of a kitchen where milk spilled and soured could be compared to the smell of a sauerkraut factory.

All things and living creatures, as well as places, have some sort of odor. We think of smell when we see flowers, but weeds smell, too. Earth has a smell. Animals and people smell.

The sense of touch refers to not only the textures and temperatures we feel against our skin. It also includes:

- body awareness, kinesthetic feeling
    tensions in muscles
    changes in respiration
    sensations in the stomach, throat, and other places
    awareness of clothing
- atmosphere
    movement or density of the air
    temperature and humidity

When you describe sounds remember to include background noises as well as nearby sounds. Also, analyze the sounds you make with your own body. For example, if you are now sitting at a computer, notice that while the machine hums, you may occasionally creak your chair, and you might sniff or clear your throat. Someone may speak to you, and you may answer. Workers beyond your window might clatter trash cans while a garbage truck whines as it compresses its load. As an exercise, analyze all the perceptible sounds you hear now; later, when you recall the event of your narrative, remember or reconstruct the many sounds at that scene.

Sight is the most described sense. You've probably shown how the setting, people, and objects looked, but you may not have described the lighting. To add depth and atmosphere to your description, tell what kind of light was present, its angle and its brightness. Mention shadows or dark places.

Taste is less frequently important in our experiences, but its inclusion flavors our writing. If your first kiss was minty because your date chewed spearmint gum, share this sensation with the reader.

Of course you would not want to include all your senses in all your descriptions, but be aware that some sensory description will enrich your writing. To select which senses are appropriate for a particular chapter, think back on the experience, identify the predominant sensations, and feature them.

Include Quotations
If you can remember even approximately what you said and what other people said, add quotes. Quotations add individuality and animation.

Disclose Your Feelings
Sometimes writers tell what events occurred but neglect to reveal what emotions they felt. To show your feelings in indirect ways is fine and is often preferable to stating them. Show them either indirectly or state what you felt, but don't leave readers unaware of how you reacted to the important experiences in your life.

Indicate the Significance of the Experience
Often the significance of an experience is evident to ourselves in the context of our lives; however, readers may not understand why the event was important. Try the "So what?" test. Say to yourself, "This experience happened to me, so what? What is its meaning for me? What difference did it make in my life?" Then examine what you wrote to see if the reader will understand why you chose to write about this happening and how it made a difference.

Make Deletions

Cross out.
Scribble over.
Eliminate ineffective writing with a few quick strokes. Eradicate verbal and mental clichés. Your creative well will not run dry; rather, you'll dig deeper to fresher water.

Make Changes

Replace Vapid Verbs With Vigorous Verbs

Verbs are the writer's most powerful medium. Choose the most vivid, descriptive verbs available. The following exercise was devised by a talented teacher, Sister Helena Brand, S.N.J.M., who taught at Marylhurst College. As you read the paragraph, say an expressive verb when you come to the blanks.

He ＿＿＿＿＿＿＿ down the hall.
She ＿＿＿＿＿＿＿ on the couch.
"Is that you, Frank?" she ＿＿＿＿＿＿＿.
"Yes," he ＿＿＿＿＿＿＿ as he ＿＿＿＿＿＿＿ her.

If you chose pale, vague verbs, your paragraph will be bland, like this one:

He walked down the hall.
She lay on the couch.
"Is that you, Frank?" she asked.
"Yes," he said as he saw her.

However, if you chose vital, vigorous verbs, your paragraph will convey more drama and be more engaging.

He swaggered down the hall.
She trembled on the couch.
"Is that you, Frank?" she whispered.
"Yes," he sneered as he grabbed her.

Or:

He tiptoed down the hall.
She crouched on the couch.
"Is that you, Frank?" she hissed.
"Yes," he gulped as he shrank from her.

Experiment with many different verbs, and revise this paragraph in a variety of ways. Then read the rough draft of any chapter in your memoirs, underlining its verbs. Consider replacing the general, vague verbs with vital verbs whenever such a change would be appropriate.

Replace General Nouns With Specific Nouns

When you see that you've used a general word, replace it with a specific word. Instead of saying someone had a dog, tell us he had a Labrador retriever. Better yet, give us a picture of a gaunt, stiff Labrador retriever with a gray muzzle or a playful, sleek black Lab. Generic nouns give us only fuzzy, colorless pictures, while concrete nouns convey clear, specific images.

Here are examples of general nouns and specific nouns:

general	specific
tree	tulip tree with waxy leaves
cake	German chocolate cake
song	"You Are My Sunshine"
coat	wrinkled, khaki trench coat
pen	blue Paper Mate ballpoint pen

Change the Passive Voice to the Active Voice

The active voice feels more alive and immediate than the passive voice. Its pattern is subject, verb, object. Here is an example: Roberto pitched the ball.

The passive voice is less dynamic. Its pattern is object, verb, subject. For example: The ball was pitched by Roberto. This voice is flaccid. Can you imagine a sports announcer speaking this way? We would not feel the pulse of the game.

Rewrite the following sentences, changing them from passive to active voice.

Examples:

A rousing song was sung by Frogel.
Frogel bellowed a bawdy ditty.
The marathon was won by Zoster.
Zoster burst through the finish line ribbon.

Your turn (remember to choose a vivid verb):

> The chocolate mousse was eaten by Clovis.
> A stern lecture was given by the matron.
> A gazelle was eaten by a pride of lions.

When the subject is not named, the passive voice is evasive: A mistake was made. Action will be taken. Office memos sometimes take this form. The passive voice is useful when the writer wants to be vague. Responsibility is avoided. However, for most writing and for writing memoirs, we want the energy and directness and responsibility of the active voice.

Some writers habitually use the passive voice without being aware that they employ this sentence structure. Since use of the passive voice is not usually a conscious, narrative choice, careful writers often ask listeners to inform them whenever they hear the passive voice. Ask the listeners in your response group to do this for you.

Replace Verbs of "Being"

Replace "It is," "There is," "There were," "There was" with specific subjects and vigorous verbs. For example, instead of writing "It was raining," a bland sentence, you could write "Rain pelted us" or "Rain misted into our hair and sweaters." Here are more examples:

> There was a dog inside the fence.

Drop "There was," replace "dog" with a specific noun, and choose a vital verb.

> A snarling Akita paced inside the fence.

Here are more changed sentences:

> There were lots of ants.
> Countless ants milled over the potato salad and fried
> chicken.

It was a dusty room.
Cobwebs clung from lamp shades, and dust dulled the
    tabletops.

For practice, change the following sentences. Drop "It was" and "There was." Begin each sentence with a precise noun followed by a vigorous verb.

It was a windy day.
It was hard for the old man to see the sign.
There was a child in a high chair.
There was a clock in the hall.
There was a mosquito in our tent.

When you are writing a first draft, ignore all these editing considerations. Be oblivious to verb and noun choices, voice, and "being" constructions. As you write, be conscious only of the experience you're remembering. Worrying about stylistic considerations as you reminisce would distract you and impede your fluency. Because you're skipping lines, you're leaving room to revise later. Step four of the writing process is the effective time to underline your verbs, replace vapid verbs with vital ones, replace generic nouns, change sentences from the passive to the active voice, and rewrite sentences that start with "being" constructions.

Rearrange Sections of Writing

You may realize that certain paragraphs or sentences should have preceded others. Fine! Circle what you want to move, and draw arrows. Change the sequence of big or small sections in your chapters.

The Revised, Edited Draft

The foregoing suggestions are basic and serviceable and are used to good effect by memoirists, but they are not the only techniques writers use. Be aware that some writers scrutinize their sentences for word repetition, check to see that sentence length and structure is varied, listen for pleasing cadences, and apply other editing subtleties. You will automatically apply many of these sophisticated techniques when you make changes as a result of hearing your drafts read aloud. However, if you wish to understand further strategies for revision and editing, see the books by William Strunk Jr. and E.B. White and by William Zinsser that are recommended in chapter twenty-eight.

A thoroughly revised draft may be marked so much and contain so many insertions that it is difficult to read. Such reworking is typical of the majority of professional writers. Literary scholars enjoy studying the sequence of drafts by famous writers to observe how their poems or prose evolved. However, people who do not aspire to write literary art do not need to revise their drafts many times. Engaging memoirs can be achieved by simply taking time to add, delete, change, and rearrange.

CHAPTER THIRTY

Proofreading for Correctness

Some writers want their rough drafts to be proofread by an expert who holds a red pen. Such serious proofreading is not usually necessary unless you plan to have your memoirs published for broad distribution or you are a student writing for academic credit. If your memoirs are written for your family and close friends, you can achieve a satisfactory level of standard English by first checking the big units—the paragraphs—then the sentences, and finally, individual words.

Paragraphs

Glance at the pages of your rough draft. If you find only one paragraph on a page, you've probably run paragraphs together. Find where your text shifts from one idea to a different one, where, if you were reading aloud, you would take a breath and might change your tone of voice. Mark those places for paragraph breaks.

If you quoted speakers, check also to see that you began a new paragraph each time you changed speakers. This is a visual clue to readers. Changing to a new paragraph is like turning one's head from one speaker to another; it helps readers know that a different person is talking.

Sentences

Run-Ons

Many people make the error of writing "run-ons," sentences that run together. An effective way to catch them is to read your draft aloud, sentence by sentence, *from the end of your chapter to the beginning*, listening to each separate sentence. Reading your chapter in reverse order lifts sentences out of their context and allows you to hear them individually. By listening to each sentence as it is spoken, you'll hear the merged sentences. This method of catching run-ons sounds bizarre, and you'll feel strange the first time you try it, but you'll appreciate its efficacy once you've done it.

In a quiet, private place where you won't feel self-conscious, read aloud the last sentence of your chapter. You'll know if it's a single sentence by listening to it. If it is two or more sentences, separate them. Then read the next-to-the-last sentence and listen to it. From the end of your chapter to the beginning, proceed to read and listen to each sentence, and separate the sentences that run together.

Fragments

What if one of the sentences you read sounded incomplete? It could be a fragment that needs a subject or a verb. Consider whether it's effective alone. Fragments may be used to good effect, but accidental fragments can weaken your writing. Imagine a stranger walking up to you and saying only the partial sentence you wrote. Would you nod or feel bewildered? Listen to the sentence again to decide if the fragment is all right as it is or if you should make it into a full sentence by adding the missing part.

Displeasing Constructions

Persuade a good friend to read your draft aloud to you. You'll hear overused words, awkward phrasings, and confusing constructions. These problems are more apparent when someone else reads your draft aloud to you than when you read it. Once you've identified what doesn't sound right, then you can change your sentences until they make sense and do sound satisfactory.

Words

Spelling

Spelling can be checked by your computer or a proofreader. If you must find your own misspellings, give your draft a cursory reading only for spelling, circle the words in question, and look up all of them in a spelling session.

Homonyms

Misused homonyms, words that sound alike but have different meanings, are difficult for the writer to identify unless she knows the meanings of the words; spell-checkers don't help if the misused word is not misspelled.

One of the most commonly misused homonyms is *its/it's*. Actually this usage is simple to master if you remember that any time you use *it's* you must be able to substitute *it is*. *It's* means "it is." The apostrophe shows where the letter *i* was dropped. *It's* is the contraction of two words. Many people mistakenly think they should use the form with the apostrophe to show possession; however, because the contracted form got the apostrophe, *its* without an apostrophe indicates ownership. For example: It's (it is) a fine day! The kitten drank its (we cannot substitute *it is*) dish of milk. Use *it's* only when you can substitute *it is*; use *its* the rest of the time.

Some other homonyms to be aware of are: affect/effect, alter/altar, capitol/capital, weather/whether, course/coarse, whose/who's, council/counsel, dye/die, sense/since, past/passed, loose/lose, through/threw, wear/where, and break/brake. These are only some of the many troublesome homonyms that complicate a writer's work. Most grammar books and writers manuals include lists of homonyms and give their definitions.

Nominative and Objective Cases

Another common error is the use of pronouns in the nominative case after prepositions, a mistake that jars the ears of most educated listeners and readers. Examples of this misuse are: The invitation was addressed to Jennifer and I. The horse was given to Carol and he. Please make a reservation for my wife and I.

This mistake occurs most often when the pronoun is linked with a preceeding name. If the other name is dropped, the writer can usually hear the mistake. She would not say, "The invitation was addressed to I" or "The horse was given to he" or "Please make a reservation for I." If you are unclear about when to use pronouns in the nominative case and when to use them in the objective case, refer to a handbook for writers or a grammar book.

Transitive and Intransitive Verbs

Correct use of *lie* and *lay* bewilders many people. If you're writing for your family and friends, proceed to write the way you speak, but if you are writing for a broader readership, refer to your handbook. *Lie* and *lay* are especially tricky because their transitive and intransitive forms shift through the past, present, and future tenses. You'll find a reference chart helpful.

Sit and *set* and *rise* and *raise* are misused almost as often as *lie* and *lay*. Review the rules about their use in your handbook.

～

These various proofreading suggestions address some of the most common mistakes. You can catch most of them yourself, but if you do plan to publish your memoirs and don't feel well informed about word choices, ask more than one person to proofread for you before you write the final draft. Most community colleges provide a writing lab where advanced students assist other students who bring their drafts in for inspection, so you might talk with the lab director about hiring one of the advanced students to proofread your memoirs if you want to be sure that your final draft conforms to the conventions of standard English.

INDEX